Big thanks to Caroline Hurry, sub-editor who was superb, fun to work with too.

Also a shout-out to all the reviewers who leave reviews for books they enjoy. Without you it would be harder for others to find the good books.

If you think this is a good book, please leave a review. https://amzn.to/3vpEFWF Thank you.

If you would like to give feedback on the book to the author send a message via Twitter to @tribalideas
- please mention the book name

Please subscribe to the authors daily newsletter here:
https://theauthorityfigure.substack.com/

Contents

Contents, continued...

Contents, continued...

Praise for How to start a business without any money

Reviews appear on Amazon and LinkedIn websites.

From Kevin Francis

***** Thinking about starting a business? Well worth reading this first...

Verified Purchase

Is it really possible to start a business with no money? You'd be right to be a little bit sceptical about the idea. But if you've ever thought about going into business for yourself...then it's well worth taking a look at this book from David White. David is a real entrepreneur...someone who has gone out there, rolled his sleeves up and actually built a business from scratch. Several of them, actually. Most of them successfully...but there's been a few "learning experiences" as well. I've known David for many years and the one thing that impresses me most is he is an action taker. He's also a genuinely good guy.

You can get a flavour of what this book is about from David's Rule #1..."First get a customer". Sounds ridiculously obvious but all too many people miss this and instead get tied up in things that take up valuable time and resources and contribute nothing to the business. The book follows on with no nonsense practical steps all with the aim of showing how to get money coming in to a new business.

So, short of taking David out to lunch and picking his brains for his enormous business experience, this book is the next best thing. Who knows...this could be the start of something big for you.

From IVANOVITCH

***** Perfect! First rate and helpful book by a terrific author

Verified Purchase

Well worth getting this concise, clear and helpful book from an experienced successful businessman.

You'll gain a lot of reassurance and it will clarify your thinking and help you save much time, energy and expense.

I like the thoughtful clarity and helpful structured approach that sets out a successful "How to start a business without any money" pathway for your own success. It works!

Very many thanks.

From Matthew Thrush

***** some good points

Verified Purchase

If you're starting a business or thinking about it then this book offers some good points to consider. While basic, it can serve as a good foundation of how you should think about business with questions you may not have known to ask.

From Shaz

***** Insightful book!

Verified Purchase

Now this is a book, I will definitely re-read in the future . The principles in the book are to the point, truthful and highly effective, I can't wait to start implementing these. Been working in the corporate world for far too long and ready to start my journey. This book has given me some good insights and I just need to take action now.

More Customer reviews appear on Amazon.co.uk and Amazon.com websites.

Good reviews help others find the book and provide a third-party view of what to expect and so with this in mind, if you get a copy and enjoy this book, please leave a review on Amazon, and elsewhere to let others know what the book is about and how it may help them.

If you have other views, or corrections to share, please let me know via the books accompanying website:

https://TheAuthorityFigure.com/

Thank you

Author's Note

Feedback from an experienced entrepreneur

Having spoken to, advised, and worked with 1000s of entrepreneurs in a wide range of industries around the world shoulder to shoulder, in the UK, Europe, the US, Asia, Africa, and Australia, I have participated in the excitement, ambition, and, in many cases, business success too.

Being an active practitioner means you are able to be a perpetual student of the game. You will spend much time thinking deeply about all aspects of your business. You will learn lessons and commit successful processes to memory.

I have noticed the difference between success and failure is simply down to those who apply themselves to genuine customer needs.

It is easy to manage from afar, or from a desk where you can control the world and manage resources. Yet repeatedly, in my personal experience, success comes from getting so close to your customer you can hear them think.

This means you must choose who your customer will be in advance, an objective many miss.

Not being one to shy away from difficult topics, I decided I should address this problem by writing out how this might be achieved. This book is the result.

You can save much time and money with this approach. I came to realize this is the 'short cut', the one 'magic trick' many will benefit from.

11

Can you really start with no money?

If you were to decide in advance who your customers should be, instead of advertising to the whole world, you would only need to address, or in marketing terms: target the very few.

Indeed, the chances are you would probably only need to focus on referral marketing and employ techniques such as word-of-mouth to get your business going.

Word of mouth is not only sustainable, it can also come with zero cost. It keeps what you do private, with the added benefit of minimizing the effects of competition.

So no marketing and sales costs need to be incurred.

What else would you need money for?

Perhaps you might wish to buy stock, invest in equipment or pay a deposit on a lease. I recommend you do none of those. Only buy stock to satisfy client needs once you have sold it. You may tell me that is not possible.

Believe me it is possible. You need to adjust the way you do business to accommodate. What happens if you buy stock and don't sell it? This disaster happens often to many. What happens is all the money you have gets tied up in stock. You will find it hard to pay back what you owe and pay your bills.

Why do you need to put a car on a long term lease? There are alternative modes of transport. You can hire a car for a day, or even take a taxi if you must.

You need to invest in equipment? How about looking for someone who has the equipment you need who are not fully using it. Perhaps there's someone who will lend it to you, perhaps you can hire what you need to get the job done?

If you borrow money you will owe money. If your business spends the money and does not make the expected sales you still need to pay the money back. That's a problem. Best to find out what a client wants, promise to deliver it and ask them to either pay upfront or pay a deposit on account.

Most business owners are glad to support new start-ups. After all, their business was once a start-up too.

Look for and act on feedback

The focus of this book is to help you get a customer and then to turn your customers into clients.

The idea of converting a customer into a client is obvious, yet it is often lost amid all the things you need to set up, run and manage a business. It is easy to get to where you are so busy being busy you lose focus. For instance, it took many years to write this book as I drew on a lifetime of personal experience to put it together. After all my efforts, the first review achieved just two stars.

Naturally, I was concerned and upset, the next day I was over it as I remembered it was not my customers' fault for getting it wrong (my initial reaction).

Clearly, I had not communicated well.

It was my problem to solve. Not my customer's problem.

Perhaps I had been focusing on the content, layout, design etc., when I should have focused more on the readers' needs.

As a result, I went through each chapter and sharpened the content to make it clearer. I added more content and detail. I have since received further feedback and now understand the concepts are more straightforward and easier to grasp.

When I reviewed the book again I found 42 growth hacks buried within, these are now included as a chapter and have spawned a follow up book. The growth hacks were always in the book, yet never presented as well as they are now.

I am so pleased I received a poor review so quickly. It led me to solve the problems and add enhancements and more value.

Not everyone wants to make a profit

Clearly, different readers have different needs. Equally each business has different types of customers.

Different readers employ business processes for different reasons, most to make profits, some to provide employment, others to communicate a message, or run a community and optimize resources.

The one thing all enterprises have in common is they all serve customers. When you focus on finding out what your customers' need, only then can you give it to them.

Thanks for the great reviews

As can be seen from the reviews of this book since, the majority are good, a mixture of 4- and 5-star ratings.

Some are eloquent and others are less so. I am happy with them all, even the 2- star rating now. Five-star reviews tell me I am doing well. Four-star reviews let me know where I could put more effort into. A two-star review with a description of what is missing provides an insight into what a reader was expecting and did not find, that too can be sorted and that is why this is the books third version, now updated for 2023.

This is just how it works in any business. I welcome more reviews! Keep 'em coming! https://bit.ly/HTSABWA your review is welcomed and encouraged, they help other readers find the book.

The bottom line is this book is not about me or you, but your customers and potential customers. It is interesting to note how often the same rules of business apply to so many areas of business, including the business of publishing.

I decided to take a two-star review seriously. Clearly the content needed to be updated for clarity and accessibility. I hope you find what you are looking for here.

Iterative Innovation

My pet subject is iterative innovation ™
It relates to the idea that not everything is always perfect despite our best intentions. By paying attention to feedback you can improve. It is an agile process. It is a better idea than giving up. It is said that most people give up just before they reach success. You can find out more via my accompanying website, https://TheAuthorityFigure.com/

The review process and my subsequent actions demonstrate how valuable the concept of Iterative Innovation can be. After all, there are many who would dismiss a negative review as a one-off and even more who would likely give up at the slightest whiff of rejection and failure.

My subsequent thoughts were maybe the reviewer was right. Perhaps there were areas I could improve.

Customer feedback is generally worth listening to. It is the best source of knowledge for learning how to improve on your efforts.

The bottom line

Readers will vary from being absolute beginners to established business owners.

I hope this book helps both.

Step one is to help you focus on who your customers might be.

If you find customers, you will find clients. Customers and clients will give you all the money you will ever need. This is a short-cut, you will save a lot of time and money if you first identify who your customers might be and go talk to them.

Employ online feedback mechanisms where possible. They are fast and often, as I found here, immediate. It is important to be open to feedback. Rarely, will your first idea be your best idea.

Customers tell you what they want, whether they are happy customers or not. You would be wise to work out who those customers could be, what their ideas are, and act on what they want. Give them what they want. Chances are high they will pay you for it, particularly if you solve a problem for them.

Focus on the areas I suggest, and you will most likely end up with the success you desire and, if you want it, more money than ever. Done well, you can expect to secure a source of income that could last forever and ever as some multi-generational businesses have proved.

A business enterprise is usually a cash generating machine. It just has to get started in the right way to work.

Hesitancies, misgivings, and worries

First, if you are in a hurry, or experienced in business, there are 42 growth hacks summarized in chapter 11.

You may want to jump there. One of those could help you straight away. However, if you are new to the business, the earlier chapters include some of the more important stories and conclusions that led to those growth hacks.

The suggestions made are not rocket science yet are often missed. Over the last thirty years, I have worked with hundreds of business owners and managers on a freelance, contractual, and rarely, on an employee basis.

The first of those rare times was when I started as an apprentice for a defense electronics company. Just a few short years later I was operating on a freelance basis advising a major accounting firm as the primary provider of entrants for their Entrepreneur of The Year awards program. The program has continued for nearly thirty-five years to this day and is now a global phenomenon.

Also, I advised and managed service delivery for the Corporate Financial Services division of a major bank.

Then, for most of the next twenty years, I moved on into the city to advise, consult and manage service delivery teams for a complete A to Z of major brands and smaller companies. From Adobe, Barclays, Chartered Institute of Marketing, Disney all the way to Z, Regents Park Zoo. These experiences took me around the world.

My training was in electronics. I knew little to nothing about my clients business. I simply tuned into their interests.

In most cases, for reasons of commercial prudence, I cannot always name names. All companies have needs and interests and you can profit when you find out what they are.

The reality is all the issues encountered occur regularly in just about every industry and enterprise. The main mission and my focus are always to grow and protect customer business interests and you can have a lot of fun doing so.

There is much to stop your business from starting properly, that could slow you down and stunt your growth. Many stop short of their potential and lose their shirts, it's a great shame, it does not need to be this way.

Growth, sales, and starting a business is not for the faint-hearted, it is not easy. Humbly, much has caught me out too. I do not pretend to be perfect. I simply hope to shine a light on the many issues, they tend to stem from one thing: when business owners stop focusing on customer needs. I learned the hard way. You don't have to.

Business can and does go wrong occasionally. However if you have a good customer attraction process, you can buy your way out of most trouble.

You can argue, as one reviewer mentioned, this is common sense. It is not, however, common knowledge. Otherwise, far fewer would go bankrupt. Major businesses bedecked with PhDs, and seemingly unlimited funds still go bankrupt.

Simply being smart and having all the money in the world is not all that is required.

The focus on time and money is often lost on the brightest and best. Some seem to think that once the money starts it will continue for ever. The real world does not work that way! The idea of the growth hacks and there are more buried in the pages of this book and the stories I share, are to help keep you focused. To help you identify the areas of common sense.

Sadly, common sense is still in short supply, otherwise, there would not be so many problem cases. This is not to say everyone is stupid, far from it. For my part, I am still learning, decades later. I remain a perpetual student!

So yes, before publishing this book, I had hesitancies, misgivings, and worries, just like everyone does. Who am I to provide this information? Well, I started in business when I was in my teens, green behind the ears, no experience, no cash, and no idea! I did not know what I was getting into, although I was right to be excited by the prospect. Like all of us, I had to start somewhere, and my 'somewhere' was as a car cleaner.

The title of this book implies that absolutely no money is required to start a business.

Money always comes from customers. No matter what you do, in the end they have to pay. If they do not pay you do not have customers. Customers are the lifeblood of any business. I suggest you cut to the chase and start by focusing on winning your first client and use that knowledge to win your second and keep on going.

I have seen too many take a business plan to the city to raise money for a business to fail. Many who acquire funds fail, some spectacularly.

When a good idea meets a customer, and the customer reaches into his or her pocket as quick as lightning, you know you are onto a winner. The time should come eventually, so why not aim for sooner rather than later?

In the meantime, you need money to live, to eat, to pay rent, or a mortgage. Chances are you have those covered already. Your income must continue to be spent on you and not on business.

You might find you need a small amount to invest, perhaps enough to buy a few books on your chosen subject. These are petty cash expenses not money you should borrow.

There is a chapter on how to earn more money just by doing what you already do. This may or may not take you through the process of incorporation, where you might decide to set up your own private company.

Incorporating a business may be your idea of setting up in business. However, millions have and, for many, this is all they need or want to do. For me and others, it is a natural stepping-stone. This halfway house could well give you all you want.

I went on to start a keyboard business while I was finishing college. It happens when it happens.

I must admit to making many stupid, laughable mistakes, I took some silly risks. However, these are not acceptable excuses.

I was 'lucky' I powered through with customers and suppliers who helped me to work my way out of difficulty. They did so as they saw the promise in what I was doing and kept on reaching into their pockets to buy my latest incarnation until one day I realized I could not get hold of enough stock and satisfy all the customers I could find. An important experience providing the best kind of concern. How will you ever satisfy all the customers?

I found the difficulties continued, a wide range of them, mostly self-induced. One classic was where I had paid for extra car insurance, just not enough, so I got suckered by an awfully bad car accident. Thankfully, no one was hurt, no arrests were made. It was an adventure, it was a close call, it was fun, and yet, embarrassing too. However, I think to be true to the reader of this book I must make clear accidents can and do happen, they certainly happened to me. Life is not all milk and honey. Things, often stupid, silly things, will go wrong.

Then, there is impostor syndrome. Well, I think in some ways, we can all think we are not worthy. It would have been easier for me to not write this book. I have had conversations with many who have a dream of being in business and they too did not think they were worthy; the risks can be large. They are the ones who drove me to write this. These are people, those with ambition, and drive who I can help. All it takes is to find your first customer. To some extent, this is a maddening reality because you are left with the question: sell them what?

It should be to sell them what you know, sell them a solution to a problem you can fix. You will find several chapters in this book to help you find answers to this important question. For now, park the question and enjoy the ride.

Once I started to write this book, I quickly concluded I was no impostor. All the stories in every chapter of the book are true.

I have more stories I could tell. The stories included serve to demonstrate the topics covered.

One last driving motivation to write this book is for when I have occasion to bump into people who are based in disadvantaged areas who qualify for a grant or some type of business funding. There are also others who are lucky enough to get funded by their family.

Sometimes, operations seem to never get around to focus on the development of customers. Instead, they are all about qualifying for the next tranche of money. The problem faced is that progress is not necessarily customer-related. My experience is you do not have a business if you don't have a customer.

Trying to contort an operation to fit into where the money is available can oddly make finance a distraction. Plus, once the money has run out, do you have the customers pay it back or deliver a return? Usually, this is the basis upon which cash is invested.

It should be a fast and easy effort to fixate on customer needs. To deliver something customers want to buy. To start with, you only need one, then two, and so on. In this way, funding is a bonus, a genuinely helping hand, instead of a meal ticket, which eventually runs out and what was given squandered. Not just lost forever. I have seen families devastated from investing in a failed business, fortunes lost.

Whatever circumstances you are in, I have found the best solution is always to focus on customer needs and interests first. Not to be focused on what it is you want to sell. Instead, focus on what a customer wants to buy. You find customers when they buy from you. Find more about them, their interests, then you can decide whether you want to help them.

I am, by no means, perfect. I have offered customers services they did not want to buy. When you focus on customer needs and offer something you think they may need a solution for, they will usually let you know why not and often tell you what they are interested in, where you can help them. It is easy to focus on a vision customers do not want to buy.

What I have learned should save you time. Everything you need to help you get started is spelled out in this book.

There is more support information, summaries, and resources available from the books accompanying website:

https://TheAuthorityFigure.com/

Most people going into business for the first time come from some form of professional background. Many have little to no experience of running a business and many don't think there is much to think about. The objective of this book is to help you build a solid, most likely to succeed, as least risky foundation as possible.

Grab a pen and paper, be prepared to work through each chapter of the book. Not for me, for your business. You will build it, first on paper. You will clarify a plan on how you will practically achieve your objectives. Chapter by chapter, you will find ideas to save you money, help you to develop the market, and discover many ways to attract new and more customers.

• **Chapter 1: The one thing you need to succeed in business.**
There is just one thing you will need more than anything else if you want to succeed in business. Many people put this off to the end. It is my contention that the sooner you get this done, the easier everything else will become. It's all you need to be off for the races and no matter how odd, difficult, or unlikely, you need to stretch to attain this first.

• **Chapter 2: Time and money.**
No one has enough and everyone wants more, here are some suggestions about how to get it. How to quickly create assets for your business to serve your position and demonstrate your value. You could start making money quite quickly if you implemented the simple ideas in this chapter.

• **Chapter 3: The importance of no money down.**
Discover the one thing customers want more than ever! Quickly test the three areas most likely to generate cash. A surprising YouTube technique to save you thinking and writing time.

- **Chapter 4: The fastest way to set up in business.**
How to move from where you are to be highly paid and highly regarded. This initial step should also provide you with a mouth-watering glimpse into the future.

- **Chapter 5: Think big, Start small, Scale fast.**
Sales and the perfect way to sell. Have customers come to you. When customers come to you, it feels like a magic trick and yet can be very inexpensive and fast.

- **Chapter 6: What to sell and when to sell it.**
Quickly start your business when you have no money, no customers, and no time. How to get some cash in to get you going. More ways to create assets.

- **Chapter 7: Convert customers to clients.**
Even in retail, even online. Learn how to get clients, how they are fun and fulfilling, and how to show them to spend more.

- **Chapter 8: Massive opportunities for service businesses.**
Services businesses can generally be started without any money. There are some which could require capital investment, yet many do not. Focus on these to get started and you will not have to worry too much about starting with a lack of cash.

- **Chapter 9: How to ask for new business.**
Discover how to talk to new customers and the importance and value of a sales system. You will find examples you should use in your practice.

- **Chapter 10: How to write an ad for your business.**
The idea of writing an advertisement is to work out in writing what it is you are selling and how you might sell it. There is a structure you can follow. Following the suggested structure will ensure you cover all the bases. Preparation leads to success.

- *Chapter 11: 42 Growth Hacks.*

Each chapter has much practical advice. In this section of the book, the suggestions have been rounded up, examined, and built upon, so they are even more applicable to a wider range of common-sense business scenarios.

- *Chapter 12: Next Steps...*

All good things come to an end, but do they? There is more and you will discover how to get further insights in this final chapter.

Do not just take my word for it. Over the years I have worked with hundreds of business owners some long-established and some just starting out. Here is what some of them say:

"David White has succinctly summarized the chief, simple but profound reasons businesspeople with ambitious intention, good ideas, and capability get 'de-railed' from their progressive realisation of success. David is of course, an experienced, successful entrepreneur and valued advisor to entrepreneurs, as well as a gifted teacher."

Dan S Kennedy, Author, Serial Entrepreneur, Strategic Advisor

"David's knowledge in business and marketing - hand in hand, with his unbridled energy and enthusiasm, inspires all to up their game. Always something to learn and improve - and always fresh ideas and angles — always pushing forward — and getting real results"

Lisa Catto, Consultant, and Coach

"It was my pleasure to connect with David on LinkedIn and have a call over skype. I learned so much. David shared many insights which I believe will be valuable in growing my business. He speaks and mentors from industry experience rather than cliches. Very refreshing and inspiring."

Christopher Collins, CTO

'I had the pleasure of working as Head of Sales at Weboptimiser 2007-2010, and we've remained in touch. I can honestly say that I've never met another individual with such a broad range of skills. A quick look at a large number of his Endorsed Skills shows the extent of his abilities, talents, and accomplishments. A brilliant mind acknowledged expert and a good friend.'

Gary Jennings, Strategic Account Director

'David White is a powerhouse of the business invention. I've known him for about 6 years now and am always impressed by how he can take an idea and build it into something that can be used by a business. If you need any sort of new business strategy David is the man to go to. I have used his services many times and will again and again - his successes speak for themselves.'

Fergus McClelland CEO Vocaltrademark

'I met David at a business seminar and was immediately struck by not only his technical ability but also his business acumen. I have no hesitation in recommending David'

Craig Boddington, Managing Partner

'David is an entertaining and expert speaker with a broad understanding of marketing and an encyclopaedic knowledge of the Internet.'

Nick James CEO & Author

'David is an energetic and innovative digital marketing advocate. His knowledge and commitment has gained industry recognition and he is a regular speaker at key industry events and a published author of several best-selling digital marketing books. David's knowledge of the digital sector combined with his gregarious personality make him a perfect speaker'

Carla Cotterell Business Development Consultant

The objective of this book is to not only provide inspiration and motivation, but also a step-by-step process of real-world strategies with real everyday problems faced. You'll discover more chapter-by-chapter.

To your success

Chapter 1:

The one thing you need to succeed in business

If you possess a skill others cannot provide, you may have the basis to start up a business.

Occasionally, all is required is a willingness to provide what others cannot or do not want to do.

There are many reasons and ways to launch a business. You may simply be planning to add a new income stream to an existing business. You may want to increase your income, or you may want to run your life independently.

Most people think there is a single step from where you are today to where you want to be. Every objective is led to via a stairway. If your initial step is to follow this book, your odds of success will improve considerably.

Your job is to work out what all the steps are necessary to achieve your objective in practice, suited to your start-up. We might feel like jumping a step or two just to get to the good bits. Be assured, if you follow the steps and complete them, starting with the first step, it will be a steadier climb.

Equally if you take the wrong first step, you could miss the objective completely.

When should you start a business?

A fundamental question many ask is when is the best time to start? The best answer is the same for the following question: When should you plant a tree? Twenty years ago.

Some of us wait as if we are waiting for a sign from God. Some of us are waiting for something significant to happen as the signal to begin, like the sound of a starting gun. Others wait until they are in dire straits with their backs against the wall as there is nothing more to lose, so much has already been lost. Best not to wait that long.

If something does happen, great, use it. However, something substantial often happens when you start anyway, your start-up may just work.

The objective of this book is to encourage you to get started sooner rather than later. If you fail, you will learn from failure.

What is your business?

Broadly speaking, there are service businesses and production businesses.

Businesses range across hundreds of industries, from agriculture to zoology and everything in between. The business to be in must be the business you are most likely to enjoy.

After all, if you don't enjoy what you do, the chances are high you will pack it in with disgust and boredom. When times get tough, as at some point, they inevitably do for one reason or another, you need to have the ability to see things through. The fundamental reason to keep things going will be your love and passion for the area of business you are in.

Generally, in good times and bad, your enthusiasm for what you do should shine through and resonate with your potential customers, partners, suppliers, and colleagues.

However, if you turn a passion into a business, it could be the beginning of the end if things don't go to plan. Business does not always go bad. Rarely will your initial business idea be the business you end up in. You may start by following your passion.

For instance, you may be passionate at cooking and be a talented cook and a certified chef. However, you will also, in the early days especially, do much other work, and not be a chef at all.

You will discover being in business is about enticing customers and making sure they are happy and motivated to return for more.

As a cook, providing a delicious meal is the minimum skill you need. All customers expect you to produce the most notable quality food and that is a minimum expectation.

If you require customers to rebook, come back and recommend you, simply delivering the goods is a minimum expectation. Most customers will not thank you for what they expect as a minimum, after all they will pay for it.

You will need to collect their contact information and develop a personal relationship to entice them back.

If you outsource customer getting and customer management, you will likely miss a trick. If you fall out with the person you outsource to, or if they move on, your business could be severely disadvantaged. This is not a situation you want to be in.

You must have a managed process or system for customer acquisition and retention. Consequently, if you outsource a job function, it must operate and succeed in their absence. You need to run your business so replacements can easily pick up the pieces. As Chef you are not there just for the cooking.

Ultimately, whatever sector or area of business you operate within, you are in the business of customer acquisition and management. Quality control and quality of service or product is of paramount importance too.

You may think anyone can sell, and anyone can manage customers. Most managers in sales are constantly seeking people who can sell or who are good managers. Because they are few and far between. However with the best will in the world, your product and service has to be good, as clients will vote with their feet. It is very hard to succeed with a poor product.

One of the key problem areas is in sales. Particularly where the sales team does not know enough about the services being managed or client requirements. I once hired a very smart, intelligent, well-dressed, well-spoken woman who lost a client due to a misunderstanding of the meaning of the term pay-per-click. We lost the client because the client complained that our representative refused to understand what pay-per-click meant. The clue, of course, was in the name: pay-per-click.

We all thought what we accomplished was obvious, yet the client made up their own mind. It appeared to the client we had no clue about what we were doing because of what was said.

I am certain if I had been in the room any misunderstandings would have been diffused. In these circumstances, my knowledge and skill set were on the technical side of service delivery. I was Chef. Yet, the requirement was to manage customer expectations, keep them happy and motivated to continue to do business with us. Ultimately, it was my fault and my loss too, the Chef should have been in the room.

Outsourcing sales is not consistently the most effective thing to do. Yet, ultimately, to enlarge the business, it is beneficial. To outsource sales, operational processes need to be in place.

Operational processes cover processing, production, quality, security, human resources, training and much else, including sales and marketing. Issues in any area can take your eye off the ball. To hold on to the ball in play, you must retain customers as they provide the cash and the impetus to trading success.

A sales process would describe what your customer is most likely to be interested in. What to do to arouse their interest. How to haul them in. How to pitch for the service, how to conclude the deal and then how and what to deliver. All this can vary as each customer is likely to have different requirements.

Customers tend to be clear about what they want, and tell you what they are interested in. This may lead you towards an undesirable area of business you do not desire to promote. For instance, you may be a specialist pastry chef (to continue the chef analogy) and you realize your customers want other meals that do not require pastry.

You could get annoyed. Or, on the basis you are happy to retain clients to ensure the business makes a profit, you may adapt to their needs. My recommendation is to adapt.

Business success is all about supplying customers with what they want, it is not usually exactly what you intend to provide. Customers may not care about your credentials. Customers simply want a good product and prompt service. Due to their lack of knowledge, customers can't describe their needs, yet they often know what they want when they see it!

So, to some extent, running a business is an experiment. It may be that certain customers are interested in your headline area of expertise. They introduce others and don't explain what you do or who you are. In this way, their colleagues assume you are good, because of a recommendation, and then try to fit you into their model of the world. Unless you can educate them otherwise. In the case of the credentials of a chef, your menu could provide the education necessary.

If you are really stuck for ideas as to what business to start, there is a very old book called Discovered, 505 Odd Enterprises by George Haylings. The book is packed with different business ideas ran over the years which may inspire you. However you really want to be in the business of matching customer demand.

When it comes to running a business, you will want to create business processes across the board. You will want to ensure the business runs smoothly, from sales to production to delivery to finance. First, you need customers.

You will need to work out what customers want, and you will need to work out how to give them what they want in a way they want it. Plus you need to make them happy too.

First, the one big thing you need to get started, before anything else, is a customer.

A successful business needs customers, in the beginning, and on an ongoing basis. Your first mission should be to do what it takes to get your first customer. There should be nothing to restrict you from first seeing if you can discover a potential customer. It is not enough for a potential customer to say they are interested. You must find a paying customer. A customer is someone who pays. Only then will you have the potential to build a business. Many say what they want and then don't buy.

To get an initial paying customer, you need to offer a very simple service or product. It must be a product or service you can deliver to someone in return for payment. In many cases, the offer may simply be an advisory service. An advisory service is possibly the quickest way to start a business, as the only other thing you need is your experience.

You could get paid to train, consult on, or describe how to perform a task. Perhaps so your customers can perform the task themselves, or perhaps consider further investment to fund the development of a product or service tailored to suit them.

Sadly, 60% of all new businesses fail in the first three years. Most in the first year. Usually due to a lack of a business plan, cash flow problems, or a lack of understanding of business concepts. All three issues are addressed in this book.

To hammer the idea home, the first business concept you must understand and accept is that you only have a business when you have customers. Everyone and anyone could become a customer or be connected to others who could become your customers. As people are everywhere, you need to go look for those who look the most likely to become a customer.

David Whites' Start-up Rule #1
First Get A Customer!

Many think it is impossible to get a customer if you don't first have a product, or service ready to sell. This can be the beginning of a set of reasons to persuade yourself why it is impossible to get a customer until you are all set up. A mistake.

Certain businesses need capital to be injected to start. These, by definition of this book title, must be excluded from possibility. You cannot easily start a business requiring capital invested if you do not have any money to invest. It is possible, you could borrow it, yet most investors in a business venture will require certainty, surety, and assurances to protect their money. Chances are you will end up not being the owner of a business, but a partner or employee. This book is not for you.

This book is for those who do not have a significant amount to invest and are not particularly keen on getting into debt. Personally, I would never recommend taking on debt to start a business. If the business failed, stalled, or stopped for some reason, how would you repay the debt?

The idea is to find a customer , make a sale and get paid. This way your customer provides all the working capital you'll ever need, you will have no debts to pay and you will build up capital. It is admittedly a simplistic approach and yet it is one with a lot of merit. There are many businesses started this way and once you are running you can use the money you earn to invest further as you wish.

Essentially you should know a customer is someone who needs a problem solved. Our objective is to let them know we have the skills and ability to fix it. For this service, there is a cost and if we deliver on our promise, they agree, in advance to pay. This is not a personal demand, this is the way it has always been.

I have found prospective customers are very keen on getting their problems solved and will, on many occasions, pay up front, sometimes all, sometimes a percentage.

Online, most customers pay up front.

So, if our first objective is to find a customer, we need to think about who our potential customers could and could not be. By understanding who our customers are not, we narrow the focus. We will find we can eliminate certain sectors of the market. We save time and increase our chance to find fee-paying customers.

Cash flow is probably the most concerning issue for a start-up. It is easy to turn to credit cards or bank loans. These are to be avoided, as they quickly run out and need to be repaid. The best way to avoid cash flow problems is not to spend any cash. You should not lose what you have not got.

The very best way to avoid cash flow problems is to get fee-paying customers. Ask them to pay before, after, or during your service or product delivery. You dictate your terms of business.

This is not fiction. I am not a reporter or a journalist, and I write from actual, first-hand experience and knowledge. I have more experience of starting a business by finding customers than writing about them. Usually, it seems, it is the other way around. You make it clear you are starting up and you need to be paid to help them achieve an objective and solve a problem.

You should have already agreed the price, all we are really talking about now is the timing of the payment. Most will be glad to help themselves, especially if they know you are starting out and investing time to specifically help them.

Confidence, consideration, and respect surround the successful business person. You will bear the look of prosperity and success as soon as you win your first customer. It is transformational.

Therefore, it is important to imagine what a customer looks like and to think through the process of what your customer would want.

Prepare to deal with objections and overcome negativity to land your first customer. You can ensure you do not look vain, desperate and feel broke if you vividly imagine having just won your first customer.

Imagination is not the solution. Imagination is simply a way of getting into the mood, to assume the position. You still need to win over a customer.

The benefit of winning your first customer is not just the money. While money is essential and part of the transaction, the bigger reward will be your pride and how you feel. You will forever know what you need to do is possible, on the basis you have done it. You will also know what to do and know you can do it again.

Starting a business without any money is, hands down, the safest way to start a business as there can only be an upside. After all, the purpose of a business is to make money.

If you put money into a business, especially at the beginning, chances are you will lose it. It is not about being cheap. It is about playing safe. I recommend you get customers first for this very reason.

Invest when you have a business generating cash. Use the money the business generates to invest in the business. Grow the business once you have proven the business works, and you are happy to move forward with it.

Your business does not have to be perfect first time around. Only practice makes perfect everyone appreciates that.

Some invest in a business because it satisfies their dream and then discover they don't enjoy it. For instance, during the lock down, many sold their city houses and bought farms in the countryside. Farm prices sky rocketed due to demand, and many made huge investments. Only to discover, when they got there, they did not enjoy living on a farm and yearned to live back in the city.

The objective is to show you how to fish, so you can fish again as often as you want. If you need more money, you must possess the required skills to go back to the fountain of customers where you will find more money.

Build your business on a solid foundation

If you are planning a start-up or if you have a new business, there are important considerations.

Having worked with thousands of entrepreneurs across the world in all sorts of industries. I have heard of many exciting ambitions and, in many cases, successes too. I have noticed that those who succeed are genuine students of their game and spend time thinking deeply about all aspects of their business.

However, the difference between success and failure is simply down to those who focus on customer needs and those who don't.

Focusing on the customer first, means you are not focusing on spending money on equipment, leases, making capital investments, hiring staff, securing your location or anything else.

One of the most common family investments before the pandemic was to invest in a restaurant. Families would club together to create a pot of money to secure a leased location or buy a property, then to fit it out with all the latest kitchen equipment. This takes time to organize, too. So much effort and all without understanding what the customer wants.

A great place to buy kitchen equipment cheap is at an auction. Unsurprisingly, this is because most restaurants go bust.

How to start your business

Most often, I hear people want to raise money first. Or, they have spotted an idea, think they need to be an authority and so they decide to get qualified. Well, don't let me stop you if you can get a qualification, go for it. If you can raise money, great. Just remember you must focus on customer needs.

The first key is to find a customer.

I suggest you find someone who needs your help and help them. If you are a chef, cook great food and find a customer who is prepared to pay a chef. Do you really need a palatial restaurant before you get your first customer?

Location and ambience can help, just remember you don't have to take a lease, you don't have to buy the property. There are customers who will pay for a chef to come to them. There are plenty of people who pay to be taught by a chef. When you are getting started, think fast and low cost. What can you do at low or no cost to generate cash?

You can offer help to potential customers at a special rate. Essentially, the fastest way to start a business is to start. More than anything else, you need to help some customers who know what they want. You only think you know what they want.

Most initial business ideas are rarely the businesses you end up in. All businesses change over time to adapt to customer needs. Expect change to start from the beginning. Think about what you can change so potential customers will see you as someone who is open, different, and likely to be a better fit.

For example there are several very successful so called 'flying' chefs who come and cook amazing high quality meals using your kitchen, at your home. Especially for those entertaining guests, where the chef becomes the celebrity of the evening.

The second key is to be very clear with your customer.

Be honest, tell your potential customers what the deal is, tell them why you want to help, tell them how you can and can't help. If, after all that, they still want to work with you, great.

Don't tell people you can guarantee success if you don't know what success looks like to your customers. The key is not to make promises you can't deliver. If anything, under promise and over-deliver. Over delivering is what will help you to build a reputation, how you will get business by referral. In the early days, you need all the case studies you can get as these prove and demonstrate to others you can do the work.

The third key is to set your terms.

This is part of being clear with your customer. This part, the money part. If you plan on charging.

Lots of people want help, ultimately, you want customers prepared to pay. There are various ways to ask. Perhaps you need costs covered, you need a deposit, or straightforwardly, you are glad to help, but your service and your time need to be paid for in advance.

You can set a fee for all the work. You can set an hourly or daily rate. It's up to you. You can specify a minimum or maximum in terms of hours or rate of pay. You decide or negotiate.

You agree a deal with a prospective customer and this lets them know something needs to be paid at some point. If there is an upfront payment required, then don't start until they have agreed to pay you upfront.

It is always a good idea to have your customer's agreement in writing. In a restaurant, for instance, your prices and food items tend to be laid out on a menu. Your customer can see what to pay in advance, in writing.

You should never be afraid to ask for the order to proceed. In a restaurant, orders are normally taken by a waiter in writing. The waiter confirms the order before placing the order in the kitchen. In other businesses, you might have a discussion and then confirm by email what you think you have agreed. This is the basis upon which you are going to carry out the work. As agreed. This is normal.

When you become more established, you will have terms and conditions published on your website. You will write out contracts for clients to sign and ask for purchase orders. Established businesses do these things as standard. You can do them too if you want.

These three key steps are vital when it comes to starting a business. Going through them may cause you to update your ideas and process. Just remember, most customers want you to tune what you do for them.

Avoid providing free service

The provision of services to a prospective customer for free could be very foolish and expensive.

Offering a free taster is often considered an option. First time authors also tend to give their books away for free. Be aware you may attract the wrong kind of customer, the kind who never expects to pay. Plus, if there is no charge, then there may not be a clear order. If there is no clear order, it is likely there is no clear definition of what is expected. As a result, it may be impossible for you to complete the task. The 'customer' could just keep asking for more. I know this. I made this mistake when I first started out.

The other consideration is that if you don't value what you do then why should a potential customer?

The clue is when a new prospective customer demands that your first piece of work should be free. The prospective customer may claim this is sensible given they do not know you and do not know if you will deliver.

The best thing to do if you must oblige them is to offer one-hour, or a first meeting, or some advisory or how-to information that will help them. Let them know if they want more then after that then your time or your service becomes chargeable.

Should you offer anything free?

Well, if it can help you to demonstrate how you can help prospective customers, you should.

Many service professionals provide their first hour free. The objective is to understand prospective customer needs and for both potential customers and suppliers to get to know each other. It has also caused the customer to travel to the supplier saving the supplier time and money and now the customer has arrived may be more inclined to proceed.

An initial meeting or call can take one of several directions. It can highlight a need, one not always obvious from the outset and is reached because of the circumstances, this can be very good for both parties.

The meeting may excite the supplier or the opposite, the supplier may say, this is not worth pursuing, and the best course of action may be to do nothing.

Hopefully, an initial meeting may lead to a long-term relationship and a good piece of business.

Alternatively, you refer the potential customer to another supplier who may, in your opinion, provide a better fit.

Free information

Free information may be presented as a downloadable guide, or in an interactive chart, poster, audio file, or video.

Usually, free information is focused on a given aspect or problem. It will help to qualify a potential customer, based on their interests. This may lead to greater things.

Indeed, for your potential customer, it may qualify you in. Remember, from the perspective of a new client, they are looking for a solution to a problem. The supplier who looks the most like they supply the answer may well become the selected supplier.

Just the provision of good information can form the basis of a great relationship and lead to bigger things.

From your perspective, as a supplier, free information may well be the kind of information you would normally provide during an initial meeting anyway. In this way, giving away free information online may well be a labor-saving device, plus, once formulated, the cost of supply may be next to nothing.

As a supplier, you will want to pay attention to the design and delivery of your information. You want to ensure a reader can see what your information is about immediately. You want to deliver it so it is easily understood. It should contain an offer.

Use short words and paragraphs. Avoid jargon and technical details if possible. Our objective is to impress by informing them in a friendly, accessible, open manner. Better still if we can simplify a complicated process or system.

The objective is to include an irresistible offer.

Service for free

Generally, you want to avoid working for free, however, there are exceptions, and these generally fall into the category of bulk purchases. For instance, two for the price of one, where one is free, provided you make a sale. Equally, you can make a special offer of 50% off. Where the percentage could be far less or more depending on your circumstances.

Gift Certificates

Redeemable gift certificates are excellent to offer as these are usually pieces of paper with a written value on them redeemable only through your business. These can be used in several ways. As a thank you for the business, or as a reward for introducing others, or both. This is a 'burn a hole in the pocket' strategy. We want recipients to spend the money. Gift certificates work in networking, retail, and on-site events.

Newsletters and magazines

Providing clients with regular amounts of information can be a useful strategy to keep in touch and can demonstrate relevance to maintain interest.

One of the reasons a customer buys from you is because of the values you share. They should appreciate you can undertake work they need without having to develop internal expertise, you can save them time and usually costs too.

Newsletter or magazine style communication is usually light yet punchy and highlights points of interest within your area of expertise of importance to your clients. This demonstrates your ongoing commitment and may remind your customers why they prefer to do business with you.

Nowadays, many businesses distribute newsletters or magazines electronically. This may be less expensive to do, however, a lot fewer people will read them. They are easily lost among all the other emails your clients must deal with. Instead, they take the time to print off copies and send hard copies by post. Chances are you will be very pleased you did.

In addition, having your own publication can provide the opportunity to continue your social connections with customers. A newsletter can also celebrate social events. You can even use it to invite people to birthdays, trips, or other events. A newsletter usually provides other entertainment, too. Even puzzles and jokes are well received. There is lots of software to help you create these.

Ongoing content strategies

In simple terms, just one story per week may be enough to populate a newsletter or to create an ongoing flow of free information.

Each can be published on your website and drive SEO, too. Weekly story creation offers the opportunity to tap into current events where you can take a recently reported news item and add your commentary.

You can highlight the source and repeat key facts, careful not to plagiarize the original story. All you need to do is to add your own opinion of what the story means or how recent events could be useful to know.

There are always new things going on. Often, you will find business sections or even Google can provide links to relevant stories for you to review. Reference to these stories and events can appear in your newsletter and magazines.

At any rate, monumental events occur in newspapers every day. It is very possible to link your interests, ability, and achievements to an ongoing cause like climate change, for instance.

It is reported, for example, CNN will be focusing on climate change for the foreseeable future. Other broadcasters appear to be following suit. It is cynical, perhaps yet popular, most of us appear to be interested in learning more about it.

Climate change has been fermenting since the 1800s. It is a story with long legs. It pulls at our existential heartstrings. It is big enough to affect everyone.

There appears to be ample opportunity for us all to do our bit to support the halt to the decline of our planet.

There are many other stories reported every day in the news which may be more relevant to attracting the attention of your future customers. There are many reasons for starting a business. Any event may trigger your need to start.

Most of us possess an interest, hobby, or profession others might share. This could be reason enough to start a business. My first 'real', legitimate business came about because of a home computer hobby when I was young.

Over a short period of time, it happened to make good money too. A short but quick story: As a result of a conversation with a dentist, I learned how to help other dentists move from patient care to practice management. There was no need for me to know anything about dentistry. This did not stop me from advising dentists and being paid for my time.

An experienced dentist can easily support other practitioners because they have worked as a dentist for 30 or 40 years. It is a classic path, yet most do not see the obvious opportunity to train others when you have experience in the industry.

Without any subject matter experience, it is possible to advise those who do.

You don't have to have any experience at all in anything to start up in business.

You do require one thing: a customer.

If you advise, dig holes in the ground, stack shelves, or deliver goods, someone will reward you.

Anything and everything is possible.

Start soon

When starting a business, most people spend cash on things they do not need.

Do you need business cards, a new phone, an office, a car, or a photocopier? Many of these require a monthly commitment. You may be able to make the initial payments.

The trick is to maintain them.

You need a monthly, ongoing income to cover the costs. Otherwise, your business will become a hot mess.

However, who are you working for?

Yourself or finance companies?

It is the perceived cost of business, that puts most people off. You just do not need most of them, not to start with anyway.

You can rent an office by hour.

You can pay for photocopies when you need them.

You can take an Uber.

You can hire a virtual assistant and pay for just what you use.

You can get a business card designed at fiverr.com and so on.

My first business started with a borrowed bucket and a sponge, literally.

As a teenager, armed with that borrowed bucket and sponge, I set out in search of customers and found them just doors away in minutes. The point is, you don't have to borrow money, you can borrow anything and everything you need to get started. You don't have to spend any money at all.

It is possible to graduate to consult with major brands and household names from nothing. I did it. I started from scratch. However, the one thing I felt I had to buy was a suit.

If a business is a business, it will make money. So, the test of a business is does it make money? If you cannot work out what to charge for, you have not got a business yet.

Hang in there, Rome was not built in a day, you will work it out and you will find yourself with a business.

There is a time and a place to put money into a business and the first money, ideally, should be to generate profits. We might put money into a business because we seek a return on investment, but what if the business goes wrong? And how much money should we invest? Or risk? The idea behind a no money down business is to reduce the risk to zero from the start by simply not investing any money upfront.

If you can do this, you can be much more nimble.

The tendency, if we invest money into something, is to channel all our energy into getting the money back. Yet what if our potential customers do not want what we are trying to sell them, as is usually the case, **then what?**

Paid for learning

Restaurants are very popular family businesses. It makes sense, as everyone wants to eat. We are keen to share our culinary delights. I am aware of many families, aunts, and uncles all chipping in to fund a family restaurant only for the restaurant to go bust.

Restaurants need capital invested for many reasons, and there is usually a long-term commitment to a rental agreement. A restaurant needs to fit a kitchen, perishable stock and front of house tables etc. These are all red flags.

Whether or not you have customers, you still must pay for staff, rent, and rates on a daily, ongoing, month in, month out basis. Costs never stop, and the difficulties overwhelm most.

The red flags don't seem to stop. Hats off to every family who runs a successful restaurant, it is a very tough business.

Business events that lose money are often referred to as paid for learning. Which, if you have an ongoing income, may be something you can afford to fund.

I have done my fair share of paid for learning. It is wrong. Yet it happens to the best of us. It is also a painful way to start a business. Not only do you have to get your own money back, but you also must make a profit too. Why make it harder than it needs to be?

My most successful ventures have had no capital investment to start up. However, there is a case for reinvesting profits to capitalize on a business and fund sales and growth. Even banks will lend you money to finance actual orders.

However, to take the financial risk to grow a business in the first place, there should be no need. If you have a good idea, customers will pay for it, plain and simple.

There are other issues: many will say they are going to start an internet business, for instance. A simple, common statement, yet it has the wrong viewpoint. The internet is not a customer. The internet does not buy anything.

You must start by focusing on how you can help customers. The internet is the media and the media conveys messages, customers will tell you what those messages might be.

Then, if those customers use media regularly, find out which they use once you have decided who you are going to target. If your target audience is accessible via the internet, then all is good. However, you do not want to be one of those entrepreneurs who have lost their 'shirt' on the internet because of thinking about their business the wrong way.

If all you do is read the next chapter, you could find yourself running a small business and generating an income quickly. You just need to implement a couple of the ideas you will find there.

The next chapter covers the issues of time and money in a lot more detail and answers the question: what do you really need to invest in for your business to succeed?

In chapter 2: Time & Money, you will discover:

- A simple blueprint anyone can use to motivate customers to buy now.
- **How to get to the top of the game even if you are starting with nothing.**
- Very fast methods to start earning quickly.
- **A surprising technique you can use to get customers to buy from you.**
- How to create simple reusable assets at no cost that generate inquiries forever.

Chapter 2:

Time and money

There are two things that most people do not possess for a variety of reasons: time and money.

Do not allow time or money to hold you back or deter you.

All my entrepreneurial ventures started with no money and no time. Even when I possessed time. Even when I possess money.

With each creative venture, you discover the capital you have is never enough. Likewise, with the passage of time. It is an unwritten rule of the modern business world, there is also, never enough. And there is the fact that nothing seems to move quickly enough. Patience is a constant requirement.

You would require some funding to pay your bills and cover your overheads. You never want to put your whole life on the line because you could end up homeless. This money is what I designate 'Walking Around Money.' WAM!

WAM needs to be sufficient to offset ongoing expenses and a little extra. Perhaps enough to purchase a couple of books. Enough to cover a few small outlays. Investing in a short, low-cost training course (more on this later) should remain a possibility.

You must realize making money is an arduous task. It takes time and effort. It is challenging, and it frequently takes longer than we expect. Nonetheless, the wait is still worthwhile.

Life will become easier once the business is flowing and when you get into the flow, your chief job is to create and maintain the lead generation and deal flows. There is a danger you may think you are stuck in a hamster wheel of your own creation. Again, do not be put off by this.

Believe me, if you had the choice, you would prefer to be in the flow. You can adjust while you are there. You can make yourself more comfortable. You can recruit someone to assist you. Being in flow means money is coming in. In turn, this means you can buy yourself out of trouble!

Ideally, you should try to make yourself redundant. You can focus on communicating with customers and managing money. A successful start-up will find both time and resources. Ultimately, where you spend your time is completely up to you.

Expect disappointments. You may find the responsibility daunting. However, you do not want to get left behind, or to lose, which is definite if you give up. A great opportunity is found when you find a customer. The customer backs you. You owe it to them and yourself to complete the deal and get paid.

Your independence and life itself may be more valuable to you than zeros in a bank account. If you require more capital, you must simply acquire more customers to earn it. You can have as much as you want.

The differences in time

If you come from a professional background, your employer will have taken the time to ensure certain tools are paid for and were available to you.

When you operate your own business, you need to set those things in place yourself.

The question is: do you? A start-up business encounters conflicting issues compared to an established business. For instance, an established business tends to want to demonstrate an established, proven approach. Whereas a start-up typically wants to show there is an innovative way of getting things done, may be faster, more efficient, effective, etc. The last thing many start-ups want is to look like an established business.

When the messaging is different, operations will tend to reflect the difference. You will tend to want the business to be differentiated too, so an outsider can instantly comprehend the difference you deliver.

Quite often, customers will be different too. Established businesses will tend to entice established customers. A new business will try to do business with others who themselves seek to effect change.

All businesses want to 'own' their own new business channels. Whereas a start-up will conduct business any way it can. Most often by harnessing the powers of referral.

Where an established business does not constantly want to be seen asking for business, a start-up has no qualms. An established business would pay for advertising and sponsorship, a new business may not.

1. To begin with, there is the cost of attracting the interest of potential customers and persuading them to participate in your sales process.

2. The second is the proliferation of free content.

3. The third is many of those in your target market probably do not care as passionately about the subject as you do.

As your business develops over time, the motivation changes for you and your potential customers. Initially, you will be inspired by ambition and excitement. Whereas your potential customers may perceive you as an untested risk. As you are an unknown quantity, they will need to be motivated to act.

Chances are your prospective customers will want to escape unwanted and negative realities. It is critical to recognize what they are, as your prospective customer may feel so strongly about them to offset the unwanted risks of doing business with you. With guarantees and assurance, you can mitigate the risks your customer might face with you. Hence, you need to get a good handle on what their risks are.

The key is to understand and employ negatives. We know the positives. People want to be healthier, thinner, fitter, etc. Yet human nature is more likely to take action to avoid negatives. Most do not like loss, looking bad, being uncool, being left behind, or being on the side of a losing argument.

People want to select winners. Witness all the voting polls around the voting time when the press and TV will gladly inform us who is leading in the polls. People want to vote for winners, not losers. In the days leading up to a vote, the undecided are not persuaded by facts or policies. They have seen it all, this makes little difference. Most undecided voters merely want to vote for a winner. They do not want to be on the losing side.

People are nervous about being wrong, looking foolish, embarrassed, appearing weak, being looked down upon, unwanted, pitied, or the subject of gossip. In these areas, they judge themselves by their own actions. The most successful, top-level directors are as concerned about these issues as anyone else. Conceivably, more so, as they possess a reputation to maintain.

David Whites' Start-up Rule #2
Motivate customers by avoiding negative
outcomes!

A start-up business owner can tap into negative outcomes that an established business is extremely likely to neglect. Small business typically possess agility. Whereas a larger company would employ a marketing department where marketing messages need to be passed through a hierarchical approval process and take time to percolate through to a communications exercise, if one is employed at all.

Emotional messaging tends not to be approved as a corporate-wide message must speak to a more diverse audience. Whereas a start-up will communicate with fewer people and work on a more personal basis where emotional connection really counts.

Profit from new skills

Most people in most industries are not well-read.
Once you have decided who your customer will be you can purchase books on the markets you want to sell into.

You could probably buy all you need with little more than you're Walking Around Money (WAM).

Training courses can serve a similar purpose. There are many low cost and fast training courses available online.

Training courses can be a genuine pleasure and of value. Others will save you a lot of time, provide an extremely profitable experience and make you money.

I took an Improv course once and one thing I learned was to only say yes, you cannot say no. You must respond to every statement, no matter how odd, or how much you disagree, with a "Yes. And". A surprisingly insightful exercise. It is extremely effective for coping with otherwise negative situations. Improv forces the positive and adds to what you discover.

I took the Improv course twice and cherished every moment. The main reason I enjoyed the course was because it became a lot easier to say yes to strange and odd customer requests.

If you follow through and enjoy a course, the chances are high you may get to a point where you can provide a service for others. This means your primary business could become a 'done-for-you service' where you provide what other members need.

"Done-for-you" services have proven to be extremely popular. You can command a premium for them, and there are all sorts of pleasant spin-offs and opportunities to include more services.

In addition, training courses could provide a convenient source of customers. As members of a really good book publishing course, members were encouraged to set up a mastermind group and set personal challenges. Afterward, we demonstrated the objectives. Other members half-jokingly requested those services to be provided for them.

The way to employ this knowledge is to determine a training course you could attend where you are likely to provide a "done-for-you" service. There is most likely a licensing deal you can put together where everyone is a winner.

You can potentially partner with your course provider to promote your services to all those who sign up and show interest but do not invest in the course. Similarly, for all those who sign up, you could provide a supplemental income for the course provider, which would be great for you too. For you, there are zero marketing costs, zero risks. You just divide the profits and pay for those who become customers. Perfect. What is not to like!

A second reason to purchase a course is to play customer to get to know the organizers' agenda. What are they really promoting? What happens? How are you managed? How do the course providers arrange their business? What tools and systems do they use? What else might they sell? What do they possess an outsider would not see? I want to comprehend how they sell, how they deliver, and what they subsequently sell, if anything. What other opportunities exist?

You can discover many new opportunities through training courses in an up-and-coming industry. It is also possible to become a trainer in an emerging field quite quickly.

In addition to the financial benefit of being a trainer, it has been my experience to learn as much from the courses you run as your students. You can move from possessing some sound knowledge to possessing a considerable degree of expertise. It is inevitably the way. You will benefit from repetition and from the scenarios students paint and the questions they ask.

The bottom line is this: are you interested in the subject? Does it fit with what you are already doing or have done in the past? Does the subject focus on a subject of interest to you in the future? It is critical to establish a link between what you already do and enjoy. You should constantly look for synergies to build upon your area of expertise.

Develop assets to use over and over.

Being a serial entrepreneur is my passion, I constantly place people together.

When you love your work, it becomes much easier to develop useful assets.

There is so much to go wrong with business in so many ways. Try in an area of business you are most likely to enjoy or that is at least a logical progression from where you have got to in life. If things do not develop the way you want, you will be certain to derive some value from the experience.

If you enjoy what you do, then the chances are high you will see things through. I suggest you write out the steps required to genuinely support your potential ideal customer. To add further value, it would be simple enough to put a sentence or two together to describe each logical step.

As a result, you will produce a brief guide. A guide represents an asset. You do not have to be a rocket scientist to produce a guide about something you know. From a time perspective, this is fast to do, it could take barely an hour. It costs nothing and it could constitute the basis of a fortune.

However, if you are hesitant, search for your topic on Amazon. Purchase some books or utilize the 'look Inside' feature for inspiration, check your thinking. Do not reproduce the same words, that is plagiarism. The ideas are fair game, though. Best if you can improve upon them.

Assets can represent a variety of distinct things. A business process is an asset, as is a piece of machinery or the design of an advertisement. A list of what an asset could be is virtually limitless. Assets tend to be items you can document, or which are tangible and can be used again and again.

There are 'soft' and 'hard' assets. A hard asset would be your computer. A soft asset may be something you produce with your computer, like a video or a podcast. Once made, the digital asset stay on your computer. You forward it to others or upload it to a cloud player or storage device for others to access. You may demand a fee or publish it for free. It remains your asset.

Every time you develop an asset, you will always be rewarded with a sense of satisfaction on completion. You will gain more experience and knowledge in the process. You can utilize each asset in a variety of ways, as often as you wish. Assets will help you with quality, certainty, and customer satisfaction.

There is a twist to this.

Is your asset worthy?

If you develop an asset, even if you are disillusioned with it, chances are it may nevertheless have value.

Business does not always work out as expected. You might imagine your asset is not valuable enough, too simple, or not what it is supposed to be. However, your assets may be perfect for beginners, they may become part of a multi-step process for them.

Ordinarily, we often find our own assets poor, as we measure them against what we think our peers would think. The key is that our peers will never become customers. Consequently, for this reason, you can omit any references to your peers.

An asset can be developed for personal use, just to lay out the precise steps you follow. It can be revealed to customers to demonstrate precisely what you will do for them if you want. You can be as open or closed, as you wish.

Your assets could be used as internal training aids to save you time and ensure consistency. Assets could become the basis of external training packages, or you could sell or give them away as a guide. All these uses are possible, because you produced the asset. Written assets may be safeguarded by copyright protection. You would need to seek advice on how to do that in your country, although it is generally straightforward.

When developing an asset, you are not limited to producing a guide. You could make a model, a prototype, a business process, software, crafted material, or artwork. Your assets can be anything you desire them to be.

What are your assets worth?

All your assets should be valued, reported, and itemized on your balance sheet.

If your assets are written, they will be legally copyright protected, and you can promote and distribute them online.

If an asset involves measurements, you could produce tools or calculators as further assets. These are immensely popular and considered greatly beneficial by potential customers.

The question is this: will your target market acquire or want the asset you are selling? The answer to the question is one only the market will inform you of. Therefore, you had better make an offer and see what interest the market has in it. You will become informed with excellent feedback.

You can test most asset offers in advance. If you have an idea for a new asset, why not do some keyword research on Google and Amazon, see if people search for it. Consider Amazon as a buyer's search engine. See if you can discover books or related products to the topic. See what is already out there. You will want to inform your hunch and employ marketplace-derived information to identify specific potential to confirm your niche.

The worst outcome is that nothing could happen. Nothing would merely indicate a lack of interest, from the group targeted. You can inevitably make something more interesting and try again. You can also seek a more active market where there is more 'life'.

The shrewdest idea is to sell pickaxes to miners. In the 1800s, it seemed like a glamorous idea to mine for gold. However, it was exhausting work, and many died of hunger trying. The ones who made money were those who sold equipment to the miners.

The idea of selling tools still has merit today. This idea is behind many marketing agency businesses and most service businesses. This may explain why the service industry is as large as it is.

3x Your Testimonials.

Testimonials are valuable, and are significant assets.

The most obvious application of a humble testimonial is to let others know how well you are doing by sharing what you have done for others. A testimonial adds credibility due to its inherent third-party nature. A testimonial can also help your ongoing product development, and you can use the testimonial process as a sales tool.

If customers enjoy your work, you may as well request a testimonial. Make it easy for the customer to provide them. Discover what they enjoyed and transcribe it for them. Encourage customers to approve the testimonial you write for them. You will get more testimonials, and they will tend to state what you wish them to state.

Over time, you can systematically compile a collection of testimonials.

If you are enjoying this book, it would be great to get a testimonial from you, too. Please leave a review on Amazon, as this will help Amazon know this is a good book and, in turn, will help others to find it https://bit.ly/HTSABWA, thank you.

Here is the biggie: A novel way of seeking a testimonial can be incorporated into a sales approach. You can ask a potential customer, for instance, if you were to work together, what would the testimonial look like afterward? Submit suggestions and start writing them out. You will enumerate all the items a customer could purchase from you, and they will appreciate the benefits of your approach very clearly.

Using humble testimonials as a sales tool is immensely powerful. It also lines up potential testimonials down the line. Many ask for testimonials after the work is completed, ask for a testimonial before or during, and you will be surprised.

You can build on your existing assets to develop more amazing ones without losing your original. Fresh and old-use cases can be amplified by strengthening or extending an asset by incorporating new testimonials. One by one, these new angles can provide renewed emphasis on promotion.

Many of us present using PowerPoint. PowerPoint presentations can easily be reworked to suit various mediums or be exported in different formats, such as PDF. As a result, you can develop quick assets from PowerPoint. You may also add testimonials to your PowerPoint slides, especially if they come from customers and demonstrate benefits.

New testimonials frequently provide new customer insights and they can be critical to the creation and support of ongoing new service and product development initiatives.

Your cutting edge positioning

Passions and interests can lead to consulting, or design. Especially valuable if you can involve technology, even obsolete technology. Consultancy or design positioning tends to place you at the cutting edge. You should use powerful creative positioning to induce others to pay premium rates.

You do not have to appreciate everything to consult and design. You can put parts and people together precisely because you do not possess all knowledge. No doubt you will possess some knowledge and perhaps have an expert, practical view on key parts of an operation. Typically, you will have done something similar before.

You would expect to know more about the subject than your customers. However, customers are often unprepared to take the "risk". Or they lack courage, time, or capability. It can seem more prudent and, or, more efficient for them to outsource.

Current projects are enhanced by what we continue to learn over time, as our experience grows. Creating a team is all about presenting a whole greater than the sum of its parts. For many customers, this results in the most feasible and realistic approach, one they could not put together without greater time and resources than they have at their disposal.

Future ventures, consulting gigs, and upcoming content can constantly improve, the more knowledge, teams, skills, and people you connect with.

Assets: the key to time and money

Creating engaging guides, tools, and calculators will help you and your potential customers save time.

Those can be sold, and the training suggestions create more ways for any business to generate cash, fast.

You may think you need more time and money; chances are you will never possess all you need. Patience is required, and you may as well start straight away.

Making money requires demanding effort. Success typically comes by making something available or improving it. You can perform tasks that others either do not know how to do or are not prepared to do. Ordinarily, a start-up is likely to possess fewer resources, although this can be an advantage as you will only employ those considered essential, which provides for flexibility and agility.

If training exists in your market, there may be several easy wins and unprecedented customer-attracting opportunities waiting to be tapped into, training is often both attractive to offer and lucrative to deliver.

Focus on what you enjoy. Customers admire passion and enthusiasm. Remember, customers want to be winners, they do not want to be on the losing side. Show winners.

Get up to date in your field by purchasing magazines, books, and online courses. With increasing knowledge, you can develop more assets and, potentially, your own training programs too.

Collect testimonials, use the testimonials as a sales tool wherever you can. Constantly develop alternative and added value assets.

Plan your position. Research areas of interest online, particularly using Amazon, the buyer's database.

Reusable assets will set you apart, and keep you ahead of the competition. You will be better qualified as a service provider, the more you can demonstrate the existence of useful assets. There is nothing to wait for, chances are you will fail forward and that will lead you towards the success you deserve.

Kerching!

Next up: *The Importance of no money down*. Discover how too much cash can get in the way of a good business. Not having enough cash is a pain and it will drive you towards getting customers who really matter when it comes to making profits and cultivating sustainability.

In chapter 3: *The Importance of no money down*, you will discover:

- **How to get clues on what customers want to buy**
- How to present what customers want to buy
- **3 business offers you can make fast**
- Lean business principles
- **The 5 steps to no money down success**

Chapter 3:

The importance of no money down

Establishing a business with no money down is completely different from starting a business with money.

Too much working capital can present a problem.

If you start with too much money, you are more likely to fritter away money. This may be because you find yourself funding a personal idea. A personal idea is likely to be ego-driven. Having money, you may feel like you cannot fail. Undoubtedly, all you need to accomplish is to set your plans into action. Undoubtedly, the elementary part is to manage the business. Business should produce more money. The logic of money making money.

Unsurprisingly, most who find themselves in this position are extremely supportive of the mission and are all in. There is an attitude of if we are going to do this, then let us do it properly.

This was a familiar feeling during the dot com boom, where every singular idea was bound to be a success, everyone else was successful and so should we be. The general attitude of a rising tide carrying all boats was commonplace. Everyone was on the up and up! Everyone seemed to be happily amassing fortunes, yet it was principally an illusion, most were happily turning over family fortunes and 'cashing in' on the perceived dot-com boom.

When the dot-com crash occurred in 2001, it resulted in almost $8 trillion of losses. Running a service business at the time, we lost a few clients, sure. However, most of our clients were banks, and well-known retail and travel companies like Disney had an internet presence as part of a pre-existing business. Fortunately for us, we retained a broad range of diverse clients and lost very few.

There was one business I will not name but it was a website based on the success of one of the most loved TV programs at the time. There were many web-TV tie-ins I could mention from the period. This show was already in its third series. The family behind the website was related to the TV producer, and they were absolutely, delightedly, all in too.

They had the ability to carry over design, branding, look, and feel. They could use video clips, voices, and images of the stars of the show too. Everything was favouring them. They published exclusive content. The brand name was mentioned and referred to throughout the TV program while it was on the air, in the credits, and shared the same title. The website was, in effect, advertised on TV every day all week. The website had everything going for it, and it could not have been more tuned for success. It was fashionable too, thousands were signing up every day, and daily visitors were through the roof. It was by far the most popular website in its field.

Over the years of its existence, my agency's role was to direct even more traffic to it. We made sure it was easily discovered by search engines and the site was as fast to load and search engine friendly as it could be. The site was managed extremely professionally, by an extremely capable and dedicated team. They executed extremely well. The site was number one in many, related terms. It loaded up quickly, it looked tempting, it achieved everything it should. This was a fabulous case study.

However, there was just one thing it did not do very well. It just did not earn enough money. It turned out it was a money pit. The family had put a lot into it and had raised money, as it turned out, by re-mortgaging the family house.

Always financing the next big thing. Adding a top-of-the-range all singing, all dancing, CRM with integrated shopping cart. It did generate good money; large sales were achieved. But in terms of receiving enough money and gaining a return on investment, in truth, I do not know all the facts. It was a private business. I was unable to see their day-to-day accounts. The owners repeatedly assured me that all was well, going very well and they were tremendous at paying their bills too.

I genuinely enjoyed their company, and they seemed to like me too. They repeatedly invited me to their various launch events. There were annual show relaunches, and they unexpectedly retained me to speak at their events to verify the traffic figures. Every appearance is an advertisement. Delightful times. After many years came the announcement, the show was over, and the site was closed.

They never made it work as a profitable business, apparently. They slunk away quietly. I think they merely cut their losses. They were honorable people.

I put it down to the fact they bought only the best, the latest, and were probably hooked into all sorts of monthly retainers. They were not managing their business the way I ran a business. It is vital to build a business on the foundation of actual customers. Where every month we either make a profit, or, we cut back. As much as we did not want to, it was the right thing to do. The only thing to do.

They enjoyed a business where the foundation was a TV show and rightly assumed they would receive the traffic they would later convert into sales. They received traffic, a ton of it, and they made sales. I suspect there was so much traffic every month they might have consoled themselves, well, we will generate the sales we need next month. Meanwhile, they kept on spending and adding to their costs every month. They clearly got to a point where they realized there was no return and had to stop, having run out of months.

Clues on what to sell

As a supplier with a focus on traffic, we let our clients know what was directing the traffic, what visitors were searching for.

The search terms provided clues as to what to sell. However, we did not manage their cash or their business strategy.

All we could achieve was to urge and make recommendations and offer help. Throughout our multi-year relationship, we did not detect an income problem. The opposite appeared to be the case. It appeared that the client owned one of the most successful sites on the internet, according to the data we could see, and they were reporting.

When it comes down to it, the sales process is comparatively simple. You can determine by the actions of the market what they are interested in. In this case, home cooking. All sorts of things associated with home cooking were being sold then as they are today. From cookware to cutlery to books and products, many, many things, in large volume too.

Any one of these things (or all of them) could have been tested. A few phone calls could have been made to ascertain pricing and stock levels and then offers could be made solely to see where the most interest lay. You would have been unable to say there was no interest. In this case, they could have offered premium, branded products too. They had the opportunity to use the show logo and the stars of the show. I will never know why they did not make more of them.

Over the years, I have met with quite a few members of the industry who were part of a family who founded some form of start-up website. So many encountered financial difficulties and then with their new found knowledge were able to get a job working for someone else at least. I guess learning more about the digital world with a view to making a comeback at some point.

I am aware of many who went to the city armed with a business plan who never received the funding they wanted. I did meet one or two fortunate ones, and they seemed to take a route like mine. My business served as a supplier to gold miners. We did not dig for the gold ourselves. There were many service companies popping up all eager to support customers to master sales, usability, and track user behavior. It appeared everything could be managed, organized, and channelled.

The city provided customers. There seemed to be lots of money being made available for the gold diggers. Various trends took their turn. Community, health, fitness, pets, fintech and so much more. Virtual everything. Strangely, little appeared real. A revolution had truly taken place.

Our website was our shop window, in terms of search results, we were number one for decades. Trading figures were outstanding, too. A customer means everything.

Much of what was about was fool's gold. Virtual services for virtual customers. It was straightforward to get caught up in the hype, and it still is. The hype has not gone away and is as strong as it ever was, following a new trend today and evolving into a new one ready for tomorrow.

Many of the new businesses possessed brilliant ideas, few knew how or even bothered to actively acquire customers. Most believe in the principle of building it, and they will come.

My objective was to acquire customers who would buy. My test is fundamental, does a customer want to purchase what is for sale? No? What will they buy? They are purchasing something, let's keep trying different offers until they buy from me.

Our primary customer, occurred by happy accident, because of a referral and it was not even in the city. The sales director developed some awareness of what we might do through a conversation he had with his ex-wife, who worked for another business of mine at the time.

He spent our initial meeting informing me what he desired. We agreed that it could be achieved. As a result, he placed the order. We subsequently had to quickly work out how to deliver the goods. We did it.

It was apparent to me what needed to be done and how to do it. However, it was not until my initial order that I really set out to achieve what was required to be done. This was not a case of fake it until you made it. This was a case of acquiring a customer before investing more significantly. On that basis, you do not have a business until you retain a customer. Ideas are two a penny, customers are in short supply! Only when it became clear what the customer required could we start to think about how we might deliver it.

Everyone else wanted to sell website design, we wanted to deliver what the customer wanted to buy. We talked about possible outcomes, results, and invited customers to advise us what they desired. However, we were aware of what had sold and now we are enjoying the experience of working with the client and delivering the service.

We wrote out the case study and, for good measure, created a fictional use-case or two, too. To let people in on what could be achieved. We tentatively offered the service to other marketing directors and some of them nearly bit our hands off.

The work was extremely technical, and we alluded to it without much in the way of detail. Our marketing and communications highlighted outcomes and results to be expected.

David Whites' Start-up Rule #3
Sell what customers want to buy: results.

There must be demand, supply is easy, and the challenging part is demand. We could deliver many people to on-topic sites to provide information and support their interests. The sensitive part is how to convert them to customers. We want to deliver an on-brand experience. After we find out what our visitors desire to purchase, not before. Otherwise, and this happens frequently, we generate a brand experience for a brand with no customers. There is absolutely no point, although many business owners invest upfront as they think it is critical. The critical thing to comprehend is if customers are interested, how will they make themselves known, and how can we make it easy?

The first thing to do when you have an idea is to assess it as fast as possible for the minimum cost.

Online and offline, in all areas, we have to be nimble and exact.

A phrase you must have heard of is new and exclusive. This is because the offer being made is new, and it is exclusive because only one is available. If whatever is promoted, it is possible to make another and another. It is possible to design each item exclusively until it is not.

At each stage you test, you can change the offer. You change the price point up or down. You revise the design. Change the exclusivity. Take account of feedback and reviews, and so on.

3 things you can test fast

It costs little to test the market.

For a start-up without any money, there are three things you can test quickly. You can offer time in the form of personal services, you can offer information, or you can offer a finished product.

A personal service, is where you will perform a service for your customer. Initial costs are likely to be nothing. You already feed yourself, you simply need to attend. If you could hire someone, if you had a sale, you would be financing sales. If you can manage it, financing sales is rarely a bad thing. You can always borrow for those, as you will receive the money back.

In the case of information, this is usually how-to information provided as a guide or book or digital document or coaching service. Ordinarily, you would already possess most of what you need. It is typically a case of bringing everything together and setting it into a presentational form. Massive returns are possible, and you can turn pennies into pounds fast.

In the case of a finished product, this would typically be produced from parts you already possessed. Or could get hold of or manufacture them easily to order. Usually, initially at least to satisfy your primary customers, as a job on the side. This would continue, usually, until you found you had run out of materials. Or you were doing so much on the side the income has taken over and was larger than you achieved in your chief job.

Any one of the three outcomes would represent an appropriate development for most of us. This, in most cases, is exactly how an organic business starts to grow.

You would likely need some cash to finance growth, to pay for intended services over time. However, at first, with no money available, growth might be sluggish. This is not necessarily a terrible thing.

It is tremendous to have a backlog of customers. It provides you with an opportunity to explain to each potential customer your prices need to rise. You decide you cannot afford to deliver what they require based on what you have discovered works best with your initial customers. They can shop elsewhere. Or you can offer two prices, the quick turnaround price (which may include an upfront payment) and a wait-till-I-can-make-it price. Or, of course, you can honor your promise and build a reputation for reliability and integrity. You choose the opportunity, based on the probability in the circumstances.

Your primary customers could be the fortunate ones, as you may effectively be prepared to take them on at any price. Just so you can demonstrate you support some customers.

One way or another, you will get to where you need to be.

Financing actual customer sales is easier, safer, and less onerous than funding an untested business. When you are funding sales, you are past the starting stage, you are on your way.

Requiring cash to finance sales may seem difficult and painful, embarrassing even, yet it is a sign of success too. When customers want to buy from you faster than you can deliver, you have what is known as a good problem to have. Frequently, the solution is to increase prices, cover costs, and make up for the risk and additional financing costs involved in financing sales through delivery.

Did I make mistakes, you betcha! Even when I was clear on my objectives, it was possible to hire the wrong people and pay for services and equipment where they were never effectively utilized. However, I accepted no loans and signed few finance agreements.

I did eventually get clobbered by a photocopying contract my co-director concluded when I was on holiday. I was livid, although for the first few years it did seem like a prudent decision. However, I was eventually caught out. As predicted.

I was committed to paying monthly rentals and storage to the end of the photocopier machine contract. It turned out not to be too much, so it was justifiably, mildly annoying, as predicted, wasteful in the end.

Ultimately, I owned the infernal machine and sold it to a church for ten bucks. Otherwise, I would have had to pay five hundred for it to be scrapped.

I have invested and wasted small sums. More than once, I have spent over a year on projects where I invested sweat equity for nothing. The point is, as I already knew, yet somehow forgot, the only way to test a business is to see if customers will purchase what it promotes. Momentarily, I lapsed into or tested the philosophy of building it and they would come.

This is a many times proven ineffective philosophy at the heart of many failures and, for some reason, I have felt compelled to do it also.

The critical error was in becoming so cost-conscious, determined to do more and more of the work myself.

It is excellent to be cost-conscious, but in the costings, allow for the cost of time too.

Consider time as part of the price (time and money). However, there were upsides. The lesson learned is one of them. I also managed to get myself qualified in the process, as I discovered skills, I could get certified for. For example, as an agile project manager.

These new found and certified skills enabled entry into genuinely alternative markets. After a year of effort, this did provide some unexpected cash pay days.

Lean business principles

If we look at Lean business principles and agile development normally applied to software companies, the idea is to develop a minimum viable product, an MVP.

I pursue every opportunity to apply the MVP principle to the development of any business. It does not have to be a software business.

A website can be developed, designed, and configured as an MVP very quickly nowadays. A website can cost next to nothing, the most expensive part: the domain name. You can get domain names for free if you look carefully. Monthly website costs should be just pennies if you adopt server-less technologies on a DIY basis (host on Amazon s3 for example). Incidentally, if the entrepreneurial venture fails. When there is no traffic, server-less cost models mean there are no ongoing monthly costs.

A website represents a convenient way to build a shop window or demonstrate an MVP. An MVP can exchange ideas and gain traction with visitors. You can also try out different ways to convert visitors into customers. The magic trick of this technology is that it can frequently be achieved for virtually no money. It lives or fails on the strength of the offer, not on the amount you pay for the supporting technology.

Banks regularly finance customer-based growth. Start-ups, however, can often benefit from the edge of having no cash to invest, as very little cash can be accidentally lost. When you measure out each cost carefully and invest it only in exactly what you desire, you tend to get exactly what you require.

The 5 steps to success with no money down:

1. A product or service
2. A market strategy. Knowledge of who will buy and why.
3. A passion or an interest in the subject to sustain you over time.
4. The energy to put your plans into action. This requires you to take care of yourself physically, mentally, and what you eat and drink.
5. The ability to act. This is the hardest part. Most fail to follow through.

There are 3 lifestyle keys you need to consider.

1. Consider how you manage your time.
2. Embrace responsibility.
3. Only do what you believe is right.

When it comes to time, you need to work smarter to work harder, which means you must invest the time necessary to get things done. For most of us, this means we must watch less TV. Or, if our government allows us, go to the pub less.

It is challenging, as we remain social animals, we like to spend time with friends and our loved ones. Even so, you will need to invest time. You need to think about, plan, strategize, establish, and refine your future business. You want to make sure your business takes off, and your family is looked after.

It is essential to take the time to think through as many of the steps as possible by imagining how the business will pan out over time. Avoid the generic, romantic, fill up the bank with cash objectives, instead focus on process, step by step detail, what happens next, then next, then next. You will find the money will follow anyway.

How do you entice your primary customers, who would they be? Why would they buy more? When? Who would they recommend? Why would they? What incentives can you offer? What media do they consume? What should be on your website? How would you provide follow-up emails? What would you write in those emails? How would you stay in contact? How can you encourage more consumption, more purchases, or referrals?

It can be a fun game to think about all these things. What is interesting about them is that they represent thoughts, not costs. If your thoughts lead to costs, determine how those costs can be delayed. Ask yourself if those costs are really necessary? What will happen if you do not invest in them?

The second key attribute you need to embrace is to take responsibility. Success is down to you. No one else was involved. It is pointless to blame circumstances, wives, husbands, boyfriends, girlfriends, financial climate, government, competitors, etc., these constitute potentially all obstacles, everyone in business addresses them.

You are not alone. The choice is not to run a business or get divorced. The choice is to find a way to set the business up and support your family. There are compromises you will need to accept. I must admit that discovering this part was extremely difficult. Taking responsibility is what will direct you through all the points above.

It can feel isolated at times. Friends and families will most likely not be understanding or willing to compromise. You will have to show them it is for the better if you want to succeed. You must take responsibility and actively manage your circumstances. You must continue with what has gone before and move forward with a no-money-down business.

First, starting up a business may require extraordinary effort, where extraordinary is because you have not done it before. However, you must know you are not unique. Millions have set up businesses, and you have access to a certain amount of insider knowledge here.

Frequently, there are compromises that need to be made. Time must be carved out. You may have work pressures and a family who require your attention too. In principle, your family should come first, as the objective of your endeavour is to establish a more marvellous life for them. Those who are successful take responsibility and manage their time accordingly. You need to provide time for all who require it and involve them in the decisions so there is calm, collected understanding. It is challenging.

The third key represents belief. If you do not believe in what you are doing, or, if you do not believe what you do works, or, if you do not like the customer, do not do it. Stop, get out of it, do not be a false prophet, as if you persevere you will be unable to see it through. You will ultimately fail, as you lack belief.

If, on the other hand, you have difficulty and you possess belief, then you will have hope and expectations. You will discover your ability to follow your mission through. If there is an approach to business or process you do not like, do not enjoy, or find unethical, then stop it immediately. Hurl it out, discover an alternative way to not cause conflict with your beliefs. Internal conflict can be enough to cause you to exhaust your interest and lose belief in what you are doing. If the ends do not justify the means, you must identify a more effective way. Halt, rethink, retool, restart.

You will notice that money is not a requirement for success and neither does it feature in any of the keys. I have always found that money invariably comes from customers. I found that if I attend to them, they tend to attend to me.

However, when you strike a financial ceiling, you retain a range of options at your disposal. You can, for instance, take what works in your area and sell a license to a remote area. Licenses generate recurring cash income with no need for sales financing. However, they represent an asset class and more can be promoted.

76

Furthermore, most businesses do not generate any money for a long while, usually because they merely retain one line of income. However, there is nothing to restrict you from setting up other income streams to serve as a conduit to entice more customers. For instance, certain marketing channels can be monetized. Composing a book and publishing it on Amazon could constitute one source, another, maybe by running a YouTube channel, and another might be through running a membership site. There are more marketing channels that could all deliver surprising levels of income.

It is essential to diversify by creating several income streams as soon as possible. Most business start-ups focus on just one income stream. You will suffer if there is a problem with one income stream. If you retain an on-off relationship with sales. As frequently, when you are delivering, you cannot sell. It is vital for sales and marketing to occur in parallel with production and, or delivery.

A rule of thumb for me is that marketing activity should not take more than thirty minutes to a morning max. There is a leeway there. The point is to seek transitory things to carry out. A two-minute video may require thirty minutes of writing, videoing, editing, and uploading. In a morning you may get five or six videos made, perhaps enough for six weeks if you release a video each week. It is possible to produce this and set the publication date for each video when you upload it.

If you want to set up a YouTube channel, you should expect to produce a video every week and not earn any money from traffic for perhaps as long as two years. If you produce a product and you are doing it all yourself without partners, it can take a year or more. With a partner, it can take weeks or months. If you provide a service, it can take a well-chosen meeting to secure a trial contract for a month to see how it is going. Clearly, if you do a great job, it should go on for a lot longer if you have everything you require ready to go. I have my customers pay monthly retainers wherever possible as it allows me time to plan, and increases everyone's chances of success.

Ongoing monthly contracts remain the most golden things and many customers are eager to approve them as they lock in the price and provide their business predictability. Yours too. Those you can develop a business on.

A final thought on this is I would not hire anybody in my rush to develop the business. I would treat a new business as a side hustle, and I would urge friends to associate with me on the basis it might work out. I would urge customers to pay at least 50% upfront and to issue written orders too.

You can still offer a money-back guarantee if you think it would be practical, although I never have other than with online (distance sales) where you must.

If a customer is unprepared to invest any money upfront, then the chances are you may retain a customer who never pays up. Getting taken for a ride is a familiar complaint of start-up business owners. Asking for money upfront is often essential. It is usually essential for a customer to include some skin in the game and demonstrate commitment. You may prefer asking for a 50% deposit, or as a surety, or for the funds to be placed in escrow. You need to build trust. For you to undertake a project for the customer, you are accepting a significant risk. You need to be certain of a favorable outcome and for the customer to embrace the opportunity seriously.

If you have difficulty asking for money upfront, then imagine how much difficulty you would have if the customer did not pay. Being unpaid presents a severe problem for start-up business owners.

Another crucial issue for a start-up is the danger of offering services for free. It can make you look desperate, unworthy, and unlikely to deliver quality. Furthermore, if you only secure business because you offer the service for free, then you are not commercially respecting the market.

Offering a complimentary service can slow you down, as you will have to finance it or give up your own time for nothing. A considerable one-sided investment.

You require a customer to issue a written order, for several reasons. You can mount it, as it is your first. You can prove it to suppliers and perhaps the bank and even partners, who will all be glad to verify you retain a customer. In this way, you may find they are more than willing to help.

However, a written order should clearly define expectations. Both parties should employ unmistakable, unambiguous terms to describe exactly what you are expected to deliver. This will help if there is a change in personnel, for instance. This periodically happens and can be one of the principal reasons you might wind up not getting paid.

Next up: Small steps can lead to big leaps. It is time to give yourself a pay rise and a promotion!

In chapter 4: The fastest way to set up in business, you will discover:

- How to get rewarded more for what you already do
- **How to develop valuable reusable assets**
- How to clearly see your potential opportunities
- **3 ways you can set up fast with no money down**
- How YouTube can save your time

Chapter 4:

The fastest way to set up in business

The fastest way of setting up a new business is to find out what customers want to buy.

The fastest way of setting up a new business is to find out what customers want to buy.

The easiest and lowest cost business to set up is an advisory or consulting service business because it typically requires no overhead and can pivot into content creation and training too, often both.

For example, is far easier to position yourself as a dietician or chef than it is to create a retail outlet with a kitchen. A retail outlet with a kitchen can easily cost hundreds of thousands and it requires a medium-to-long-term commitment to a lease. You would not want to fit a kitchen and a restaurant with a short-term lease, as you need time to build up a business, make profits and get a return on your investment.

For most, the investment required to set up a restaurant renders the restaurant business impossible, although thousands try all the time and sadly, most fail, because the odds are so difficult with the costs so stacked against a startup.

A better way would be to set up as a dietician or chef and go find an underperforming restaurant or kitchen and rent what you need when you need it. You may be just the kind of partner a restaurant investor or owner is looking for. Also, the kitchen may not be part of a standalone restaurant. It could be a hotel or an industrial kitchen. There are plenty of different types of kitchens. You need to choose the one that suits you.

These are some ideas about how you might take your skills that may be suited to a big investment, for example, a restaurant, yet the reality is that the amount of money required is a lot more than you can either access or want to risk, both of which are fair reasons not to do it. It is much better if you can build an initial business in the manner I suggest without any borrowing, partners, or investment.

My first services business

From the outside, it looked like I was part of the company where I was based.

The reality was that I sold some of my time to that company at a lower rate and, in return, they provided me with a presence and a base provided on an unlimited basis at no cost.

I used office space my client paid for anyway. They already had meeting rooms and telephone systems, frontage etc., and so it all worked out.

It was also recognized that my new clients could well become their new clients too. A solid, symbiotic relationship, and one that lasted for a few years. This enabled me to build up some capital and establish my first real service business and cash flow.

I repeated this trick a few times with a range of different partner companies as I built up my business.

The experience proved to be very worthwhile. I was able to see close-up the operating practices of each partner and I got to see how the services they offered differed and experienced how clients behaved according to the suppliers and circumstances they chose. It provided great insights.

A simple system for getting clients

Getting clients is as simple as talking to them.

That's it, that is the magic trick for getting clients. However, you can save yourself some time if you choose who to talk to first.

For example, if I spoke to everyone all the time, I would find potential customers who had different needs, interests, and served vastly different markets. A reference from one would mean nothing to another.

Also, if I ever felt the need to advertise, I would want to create blanket coverage advertising, the most expensive of all advertising, which incidentally typically has the lowest response rates. This sets me up to pay the most and get the least return. No one wants that, and certainly not me.

Step 1 of customer getting

The first thing is to focus on who you are for.

Who can you help the most? Who would you most like to help? As once you decide, although you could change, should try to choose a group of people you might enjoy working with, as, after all, you expect success and, if successful, you do not want to be in a position where you despise your clients. You want to be in a position where you can love your clients, where you love what they do, and you are genuinely enthusiastic about helping them.

There are several good reasons for working with people you like. Enthusiasm is contagious and so you should expect to get more work, and more referral business and to get known for being good at something. Secondly and just as importantly, there is your own peace of mind, your own mental health. You want to be happy waking up and looking forward to going to work. Do it right, chances are you will be self-employed forever. It would be a great idea to focus on a business area where you enjoy what you do and like working with people.

So, your first consideration is not what you can offer, but who would you like to work with.

Step 2 of customer getting

Go talk to potential customers.

You probably already know exactly who you would like to do business with. You will have come across them in the past and you know them to be genuine, warm-hearted people, with whom you have already made friends, in some cases, at least.

Go talk to them.

Go find others like them.

Set about trying to find 10 to 20 people, although often just 1 or 2 can be enough to give you the business you are looking for. In the case of 1 or 2 people, then you will pretty much know what you want to offer and what will be attractive to them.

In my example of setting up my business within another business, my opening conversation started with the words "I am looking for someone to join forces with". These are simple words, and you will know where they have a requirement and potentially do not have the money to invest, but they do have other resources they could provide that cost them nothing extra and they may be willing to pay you either a small retainer or on a results basis.

If you are lucky, you may be able to identify a specific piece of work, they need done and they will pay you for it. You can tell them you are going alone, on a freelance basis, looking for work, but not as an employee, as an independent contractor. Many business owners will admire you for saying so and some will tell you this is how they started.

Very few, only the very rude or those will never become your clients anyway will reject you or laugh you out of the building, although there is always one or two. When it happens and it can happen at any stage of your career, just quietly, without fuss, look for an exit and then continue with your life working with people who do understand you and want to see you succeed, as most will.

Starting your practice

Working directly with customers, is usually straightforward, they tend to be clear about their wants.

Being in business is all about focusing on your customer's needs and wants. Through this experience you will acquire invaluable personal knowledge. As an adviser, or as a consultant, you acquire incredible insights.

Many significant companies love to hire consultants and advisers as this can speed up results for them too. They expect you to know what to do and when to do it. Another positive advantage is that there is not ordinarily a long-term recruitment or on-boarding process. Also, most hiring companies consider their needs short-term, or for the duration of a given project.

You do not need to purchase anything to become an adviser or consultant. You likely will not need to pay rent or purchase a car, or any other piece of equipment. As an adviser or consultant, you learn exactly what pains your potential customers very quickly. You enjoy the flexibility to react and adapt to their needs and support them to identify a solution. You can determine whether you work from home, consult by telephone, zoom, or turn up at their offices or arrange meetings in meeting spaces or hotels. You have many options, and most customers love to be led.

Over the years, I have entered many markets on a freelance basis. First, as an electronics engineer, where I took on test and development contracts. Then to project management (on a contract basis). Then, as a marketing consultant, I decided I preferred to work with people instead of machines and then I ran my own technical marketing company that combined both my skills as I felt I could understand both sides and optimize performance, which is exactly what happened. More recently, I took on cybersecurity training and offered advisory services too, particularly in disaster recovery, again combining IT with communications. It all turned out to be more fun than it might seem.

Business suited me, as it should suit you.

You choose who you want to help, where, what, and how

As business expands, you may think about hiring people to work with to deliver your services.

The first person I tend to employ, albeit on a part-time basis, is a freelance accountant. Doing your books is important and a part-time accountant will manage payroll and chase invoices for you too. You need to make sure your personal affairs, tax and bills are paid. To be fair, this may not become an issue for eighteen months or so if you were an up-to-date employee beforehand.

It is a mistake to hire a big firm of accountants, as you can get large bills to pay fast.

You really want a start-up accountant, someone like you who is planning to start out, who is also looking for an initial client or two. Many accountants harbor the dream of going alone, so, like finding a friendly lawyer, this should be quite straightforward. However, never give any other person control of the cheque book. Allow others to pay money to your bank account. Money out is something you want to retain tight and exclusive control over.

I ran one business and made a colleague a partner and gave him rights to the bank account. He then became Champagne Charlie and drank Champagne every day, almost running the business dry. A horribly learned lesson. Don't do what I did. Trust people, just not with a credit card or business bank account. I understand I am not the first person to learn this lesson and, by all accounts, got off lightly. Others have been saddled with debts to pay off. The term banks use is joint and severally liable, which means they can go after either or both signatories. So, if the other person dies or disappears and you survive, you must pay the bank.

Thankfully, most businesses are about the upside, value creation. Managing employees to match customer needs is something you learn to do and generally starts with rolling up your sleeves and getting stuck in, great fun if you find the topic fascinating. Invariably, there are even more opportunities to make business expansion discoveries.

In a start-up, the first thing you need is Walking Around Money (WAM)

As you build up your business, the sole way of obtaining money, apart from borrowing it, unless you are given it, or already have it, is to earn it.

Earning your cash is the best way to get the WAM you need as you are likely to really value it and spend it wisely, as you know what has to be done to earn it. Positively, this way, you should escape debt.

If you are unable to acquire a consulting or advisory role, then you must find a way to generate some form of income or get a part or full-time job to make sure your costs are covered. This will buy you the time to do what you need.

Perhaps you will acquire further skills and broaden your experience to move on to getting a consulting or advisory role. A small step. The fastest and most straightforward way to collect more money and to get the insights you need into an industry to develop a business. It was how it worked for me, and many have taken the same approach.

From being an apprentice, I was able to set up a keyboard distribution business.

Even as a junior engineer, in my twenties, a freelance contract agency put me on contract to Mars Money Systems (part of Mars Confectionery). The not glamorous role was on the production repair line. It was my job to ensure that vending machine money mechanisms accurately detected individual coins to dispense products (Mars bars et al).

It was fascinating for the first week. Subsequently, not so much, at all. The money was phenomenal, for three months. The boredom was mind-boggling. I soon realized exactly why they paid so much. At least, there were some other people on the factory floor. Otherwise, it was me and machines.

Another 'test' job with Advanced Micro Devices (AMD) came along. My main job there was to test microprocessors with a view to recycling (or reselling) the units returned. It was even more boring, alone, in a windowless office, all day. It could not have been more undesirable. However, the money was beyond fabulous. I stuck it out for three months.

Something had to change

Working like this was no fun at all. The cash was great, the work was soul-destroying.

Project management offered even more money and involved others. I found this much more interesting and fun to do. To my eternal surprise (as I had no experience as a project manager) someone was desperate enough to give a kid like me a job and pay a really good rate.

Freelancing delivered quick career jumps, with increasing pay and levels of responsibility. It was a rapid way to succeed from being a lowly, trodden-down, apprentice to highly paid 'executive'. Project management was remarkably interesting, highly paid, and working with people was a real bonus. I can see why so many people make a career of it, I almost did.

Combine your knowledge with sales

I offered to share an office with a colleague and contribute to the rent.

Conceivably, it would have been more satisfactory to have worked from home for a while. Sharing with a colleague turned out to be painful. I felt compelled to move on, and I took on a five-year office lease. A colossal mistake! Instantly accepting liability for a rent of 2,000 sq. Ft office for the next five years. It should have bankrupted me.

Effectively, it had to work. I remember other business owners and peers at the time would laugh as they said 'well, you are young enough to recover'. Fortunately, the anticipated loss did not materialize. The rent was made every month for five years.

The rent was made without fail, despite having to go without food on occasion. There were many fraught days, failure was not an option. In the end, all good. Never again!

All my days were consumed worrying about paying for someone else's assets. The critical issue. Be extremely wary of office, car, and photocopier leases. Any kind of lease. They are easily agreed to and impossible to terminate.

However, just two outstanding contracts out of hundreds were just enough.

One was with a major Bank, where my team would call up companies and offer invoice financing services, an ongoing contract. The other was with a major accounting form, with whom we launched the Entrepreneur of The Year awards program. Both programs survive to this day.

We called the same people asking if they would like to submit their business for an award. Companies used to love accepting our calls. We offered money and awards!

Although most of those years were spent in a state of panic, luck was with us. Hindsight is a tremendous thing. My issue, the key to my nervous misdemeanour was the number of eggs being held in the one basket.

We loved working for those two clients. However, if either had stopped or switched suppliers away from us, my small business would have been in difficulty. We gained many other customers. Most of them were smaller and had shorter time scales without budgets. Most of the other projects would stop and start, randomly. I learned a lot about the sharp tactics certain customers employed over those years.

So, obtaining a lease, from where we had been, seemed like a logical progression. Only subsequently do you experience the broad effect of five years weighing down on you, it is a heck of a commitment. Happily, I have never repeated it and certainly do not recommend. I should have bought a property and paid a commercial mortgage. Back then, I had no idea and no guidance whatsoever.

David Whites' Start-up Rule #4
Keep Your Freedom, Avoid Long Leases

What would you do differently today?

Professionally, everything changed with the internet.

You can make videos, write articles, establish your LinkedIn profile, and develop digital persona's. Keep them true. Thanks to a referral strategy fostered by content production and distribution, more inquiries will come your way. My business was transformed.

However, deciding who you are for is still the number 1 decision you need to make. Many potential customers still congratulate you for taking the initiative. You can create videos, write articles, and set up social media profiles more than ever. I strongly recommend you write a book or two as well.

Nowadays, you do not need to follow a career path. You can enter a whole new market very quickly. You can take an online course to learn a new subject. You can get some experience and set yourself up as an expert very quickly.

A good education coupled with practical experience is, of course, ideal and this can be achieved quickly too. You just need to find some people in the market willing to show you the ropes.

You just need to have enough Walking Around Money (WAM) to start. Perhaps you already have a business and want to get into a new one. You should have no need to invest a significant sum.

Much information is online and free.

You could set up a LinkedIn account for free.

You could easily find people in the line of business to interview for free.

I would look to buy books from Amazon on the subject and sign up for a training course.

Prospecting requires you to choose who you would like to do business with. This is exciting, especially if you land a customer you choose. It is, however, still essential. The more you focus on who to do business with, the more likely you will succeed.

The first thing to decide, and only you can decide this, is who will be your customer? Who are you for?

You try to help your target customer solve the problems they face. If you identify the market, you will know the problems they encounter. It is completely reasonable to write a blog post or an article on LinkedIn or elsewhere about how you would fix such a problem.

There are many sites where you can circulate articles to answer problems and on each, provide contact information. You can also tune your personal profiles on many websites to make it known you are an expert in a certain subject and seeking work. You can encourage readers to make contact. Over time, your online footprint will generate inquiries. People will come to you. It will largely cost nothing.

Hone your focus. Specialize

Rather than be in 'lead generation', focus on 'cybersecurity lead generation', name it and claim it.

The idea is to define a descriptive title to segment or position you and your business as expert and a specialist. Rather than as a run-of-the-mill generalist also ran player.

A hairdresser or lawyer, for example, it might be better to be known as an elderly woman's specialist hairdresser or an international contract lawyer. The point is to separate yourself from the normal, commodity job general descriptions. it is worth getting pedantic and exact.

For one thing a specialist can usually expect to charge higher rates. Secondly, clients tend to stick with specialist suppliers.

There are thousands of hairdressers, lawyers, trainers, website designers, coders, journalists, musicians, actors, and so on. You want to appeal to the target market you want, so when they discover you, they know immediately you are for them. They will want you and no one else as soon as they discover you.

When you look at most industries, there are many generic job titles, because there are many people with similar skills.

In business if you do not stand out, if you do not differentiate yourself, it is hard for others to select you. Ideally, you should stand out by being labelled as a specialist in a lucrative area.

My idea of becoming a project manager for electronics design project work meant I could focus on electronics design projects and get the top job as a contractor.

When I updated my experienced I gave myself a new job role, it was not a lie, I seen the work done and had performed the tasks I could perform the work and I went on to do deliver the work very satisfactorily.

If I was to market myself today for a similar role, I would position myself as an IT project manager with military clearance. This would narrow my opportunities, although the opportunities would likely be higher paid and fewer applicants would compete.

My enthusiasm won the projects I applied for. As I was clear on who I was for.

As a specialist, you will get paid more.

In turn, you will become more efficient and operate more effectively, ensuring your rate is not only justifiable but a sensible investment.

The chances are you will save your customer money, too.

Next up, in Think big, Start small, Scale fast: It is a great idea to avoid running before you walk. With all new customers, starting with the first, you must start on a solid footing.

In chapter 5: Think big, Start small, Scale fast, you will also discover:

- How to attract premium rates.
- **Ensure even more customers can come to you.**
- Learn more than others, from others, fast.
- **Be certain your customers are genuinely happy.**
- Create a better business based on feedback

Chapter 5:

Think big, Start small, Scale fast

Freedom at last

The first thing to do is to write your business ideas and thoughts down. Even if at first glance they are bat-shit crazy. Even if you simply write a list of what you enjoy. Your list does not need to be organized or connected; it merely needs to be created. You can edit later. First, get your thoughts down, even if you only have one thought.

Once you start on your entrepreneurial journey, you will be your own boss of your own job. You should enjoy the luxury of picking the job, so make sure you select something you will enjoy. Your enthusiasm will carry you a long way.

In most parts of your life, when it comes to learning, you will have been told what to learn, what to think and more. They had you. Now is the time to be free and to be free you need to focus on what you desire. Hence, it is therefore critical to write down your thoughts. Your future is about you and what you want.

The dark side

Others will tell you why and how you cannot succeed, how you are in over your head, how you are beyond your station. They may tell you why you do not deserve your freedom. If you provide business, technical or any kind of advice, who are you to notify a customer or CEO about what is best? What should I do?

You may be conditioned by your family against being an entrepreneur. Especially if your parents had only one employer or who were lifelong government employees or because family roots had always been against business, individual success, capitalism.

On the other hand, you may be witness to the waste of bureaucracy. How they seem to waste money by hurling it down the drain and investing in failing state-owned utilities, generating poor returns. Futile initiatives enable and empower collectors to hound and harass, considering you as guilty until proven innocent.

There will be dark times ahead. There will be times of doubt, times of frustration, and times of unhappiness. Fortunately, they tend to be short-lived. It helps if you enjoy what you do. Why not at least think about starting in an area you know you will enjoy? See if you can combine what you enjoy doing with what you ultimately decide you are going to do. Enthusiasm is extremely necessary during the down and dark times.

Incidentally, if you have been in a certain profession for many years, a dentist or lawyer and you enjoy operating a practice. Why not lose the overhead which has been the cause of so much anguish and switch to consulting and helping other dentists run their practice? Or offer a consultancy package to encourage firms to attract potential customers or patients.

Most importantly, you must stay optimistic. As one door shuts invariably, two new doors tend to open. It is never what stops you which makes a difference, it is how you overcome it. Whenever something happens, not necessarily bad, perhaps surprising, habitually think: how do I make it work?

When you first start out, it is reasonable to take everything to heart personally. You may wonder, "why me and oh, no! Not again". That serves just one purpose: to hinder. It is the most straightforward thing to completely give up. Alternatively, you promptly forget about being upset when you accept that some things can go wrong.

Accept if anyone is to blame, it should be you. Take responsibility. The sooner problems are fixed, the better. In any case, you will have to pay the price, and the quicker you can get back to doing the good stuff, the better. One of the earliest realizations is that you can buy yourself out of almost anything.

You can buy yourself out of almost everything, including bad taste. Like all the other unpleasant things you may well expose yourself to, adjust the course, move to the side and jog on.

When things go wrong, there is no point in laying blame, wholly accept it and keep moving forward, find a way over, around or under. Provided the cash flows in, you can settle the bill and get on, move forward. Shit happens. Especially as an entrepreneur.

The vast majority of people in business are all good. This is critical to bear in mind when you go through a rough patch. Hold your nose, make sure you do not cave in too early, unexpected pressures naturally arise.

How To Think Big, Start Small And Scale Fast

We can all think big, but rarely, in the first instance, will we start big.

We typically start small or target stepped achievements. The fastest scale is achieved when you can persuade clients to pay upfront. Online is mainstream, people expect to pay upfront for goods and services. Most of the spectacular growth in recent years has happened online.

Generally, starting small means we are seeking to approach someone we can surprise and delight with our skills or abilities. Having encountered one, it is more straightforward to imagine there must be more. We start by targeting just a few.

We may come up with a big idea, let us say we develop an internet sensation with enormous potential, which still makes sense to start small. With small, one on one, you can expect and generate feedback to tailor and tune what you do.

David Whites' Start-up Rule #5
Seek feedback. Tune and tailor

It is vital to take the time to ensure you have a solid, quality, reliable product, or service to get the job done and keep customers happy. This way, you can scale the business up to meet customer needs.

Without a definite good product or service, you may find yourself in deep trouble, quickly. In the short term, you will most likely only satisfy a few small clients in any case. To grow, you will have to reshape your offer completely. Your first clients are likely to be willing to take a chance. Look for keen, enthusiastic supporters and early adopters. They thrive by being on the cutting edge and they may represent as much as 20% of the market.

After a while, your clients will become more mainstream. They are likely to require fewer personal connections and entertain more commercial expectations. They may comprise as much as 60% of the market. They merely want to get the job completed.

Next there are the laggards, probably the last 20% of the market. They demand everything, proven, and with cast-iron guarantees and are willing to pay the lowest price. You will probably love these customers the least!

You may find some customers will stay with you for years and years even though they come from each group. Each group invested in you for diverse reasons. The first group may perceive many changes in you and perhaps even reminisce about the way things were.

You will find yourself needing to identify and manage each customer group according to their view of you. If you deviate too significantly from their view, it could be enough to consign them to look elsewhere to plug themselves into something new.

It is critical to look after past clients, otherwise, you could simply be warming up the market for competitors to get in.

On this basis, mass marketing is exceedingly delicate. One of the biggest online software suppliers is the software company Intuit. Intuit sells big yet focuses a lot on small. They have a 'follow the customer home' program, where they work with customers to understand use. They elicit feedback in this way to improve their software on an ongoing basis.

You might think there are some exceptions to the rule. Consider Kentucky Fried Chicken (KFC). There are many KFC outlets around the world. Many fast-food retailers use the words 'Fried Chicken. They tend to look the same, and their products probably taste the same too. It is just breaded chicken after all.

However, it is difficult to protect most businesses. They are easily copied and even though the KFC formula may be subject to copyright and is 'special'. It has not prevented others from selling chicken essentially produced and offered for sale in the same way.

Those businesses routinely employ similar colors of Red and White and feature an elderly gentleman wearing a white beard, perhaps with a red and white American style hat. Next there is Coke and Coca-Cola, more 'secret' recipes, especially as they used to contain cocaine and now, by law, cannot.

Personally, I prefer more limited markets where there are just a few who invest frequently. Rather than the many who spend comparatively little. However, if you go back in time, these massive chains each started out as one store outlet.

Who are you for?

There are many narrow groups, who have extraordinary spending power.

It is a shrewd idea to identify these intimate groups as this will likely aid you in retaining them over time. As far as possible, you want to be seen by customers as being for them.

Being for someone requires an appropriate degree of customization and has the advantage of ensuring you remain your market first choice. You can develop custom assets to produce unique intellectual property (IP) especially for them. In effect, this process will allow you to dig a moat around each group of customers to make it hard for competitors to cross.

When you decide who you are for you will get to know specific customer needs. This focus will help you to demonstrate insider knowledge that potential customers will recognize and respect. Customers will always prefer 'insiders'. They universally believe that this will be more efficient for them. If you can demonstrate your affinity and capability, your target market will want you to steer them to success.

Your specialist knowledge, capability and experience have the advantage of restraining customers from straying as they will not want to miss out. You can build on this natural mysticism to make it difficult for customers to operate a copycat business unless they are under license.

Licensing is one of the fastest ways to grow. Everyone gets a win-win. There are two significant advantages, first it is an inexpensive form of marketing, and second, it tends to be private. Two big advantages for any start-up. It maximizes income and profits while not letting the cat out of the bag.

You can adopt these principles and apply them to almost any business. The principles described are applied to most start-up ventures or market opportunities with a few exceptions.

Avoiding Risk

Most of the extremely high-value markets, worth millions, are typically high risk with exceptionally low margins.

With vast amounts of money in play with correspondingly low margins, expect stress. The slightest error can mean you have to pay the difference. Many give up on certain businesses purely due to stress levels being abnormally high, usually because of the amount of money at risk.

Big numbers are practically always of interest to those who value vanity. More money can be collected with smaller customer projects with the added advantage of reduced risk. Lower amounts at risk, spread across many customers, could mean if a disaster occurred, it would not be the end of the world as we know it.

Any loss is to be avoided, yet a minor loss would mean a fractional, temporary reduction in profits compared to an all-out disaster. Clearly, it is best to eliminate risk altogether, where possible.

The bottom line is that you can have a more comfortable, less risky life through a broader range of low-risk clients. Otherwise, you could be many years into a business where one enormous 'dead-cert' gamble can lose all the profits made to date.

Equally, you need to do more than one thing at a time. Maybe three or four. The most straightforward way to do this is to start by focusing on one area which interests you the most. Then, extrapolate out to suit one or two or more diverse markets.

For instance, you may want to monetize a podcast.

- Take your favorite subject and target three related audience groups.

- Offer three types of products: a starter package, an ongoing month to month package and a top end package, each at different price points.

- Each package would largely be the same for each market, and the difference could merely be a name change. Ensure the name of the package suits the target market.

Take a moment to write down how you would monetize a podcast following this model. Then, let me challenge you to plan your podcast and see it through.

This approach costs nothing, yet helps you to develop an attractive offer in more ways than one. This approach to sales will drastically increase your chances of success and reduce your exposure and risk.

It costs nothing, is fast and it will also mean you will be less reliant on one type of client, one form of marketing, and one form of delivery. You will rapidly discover where your potential clients are, and you will be protected by multiple income streams.

The idea of monetizing a podcast is the tip of the iceberg in many ways. For instance, you could run a podcast alone or you could interview an expert. You could transcribe the audio and edit the content and then use it in a guide, book, or as part of an online delivery. This topic, its' applications and income-producing ability is covered in more depth within the members' area, online.

Risks in business constantly need to be assessed. Increasingly, one becomes more risk averse over time. The worst number in a business is one. One market. One service. One client. One boss. One invoice. Why take on high-risk clients or projects where you get to bet all you possess on a favorable outcome? Especially if it is a sure-fire, absolute guaranteed outcome.

Do you like your sleep? When there is only one, you face maximum exposure. Yes, you need your first customer. You should quickly endeavor to get your second, third, and fourth. All you need to do is widen your aims. You know you can do it, you got the first, so go get some more.

Scale

Scale, to me, means making enough money and more.

How much is enough? Well, sufficient surplus to requirements. Scale principally refers to the idea of generating more sales easily, and the best way is to employ assets systematically and look for synergies.

Business boils down to adding value. It is unnecessary for us to fix problems personally. It is enough to know someone who can. Are there others who need similar support? What else can we help our target market with? Ideally, we want to grow by the power of three. Work out which are your three top priorities, systematize them. Make it happen, then move on.

Looking for what customers want, or where they have pain or difficulty becomes easier with time. You will become more competent at seeking these as you become more practiced. It becomes more straightforward to acquire a view of the opportunities as your experience grows.

For scale, it is typically most beneficial to focus on being the supplier of pickaxes to gold miners. Let others be pioneers. Focus on an area of intense interest and help people with their interests. For instance, bitcoin. You may find it more lucrative to help bitcoin investors, rather than be a bitcoin investor yourself.

There is consistently a top 20 percent of high-paying clients in every market. These will be those you get to know very well, and they will become self-evident. A business requires a sales filtering system to better select the most appropriate clients to work with.

For example: as an author, you merely compose a book once for thousands to be sold. Thousands will visit your websites. In the same way, site pages are coded, once done they rarely need to be coded again. Of those site visitors, some acquire what they desire, and, of those, some may want more from you. You should enable the self-selecting 80:20 rule.

It is preferable for clients to come to you. By outsourcing resources, time, and money are less likely to be stretched. Book sales remain a leading example of outsourcing. Amazon promotes the books. Amazon gets paid a cut of what they can sell. It works efficiently. Amazon does marketing and promotes books to visitors, collects money, delivers the book, and pays out what is left. All things considered, it could be thousands a month. A lead generating passive income.

Passive incomes are ideal. Book sales enjoy the other benefits of directing customers to you. There are many people looking for passive income and right now it is staring you in the face. Everyone writes. Making money through Amazon is an extremely straightforward way to produce a passive income, it is relatively straightforward, and it can make sense. It can also encourage people to form a queue to come and see you.

Passive incomes and becoming an author are both scalable. Although it is not the only activity to focus on. For instance, if you interview experts, you will learn more about your target market, create content for a podcast or similar.

Aim to produce content you can use in many ways. Use the same content in advertisements, special reports, video, online and print articles, and online membership areas.

Making money by writing is an essential skill. Before my first book, I had known technical authors, I had known copy writers who wrote advertising marketing stories, direct mail, and brochures. They never taught me how to write! It was a skill they kept to themselves. However, it was important to read, and observation can go a long way to pick up the skills. Start collecting items of interest for your own future reference. Writers start by being avid readers.

Social media posts, emails, and post replies practice writing. We all read; we all write. Writing a book is about writing in a coordinated way, about one or two of your favorite subjects. Writing is also quiet, peaceful, and costs nothing to speak of and there is hardly any stress involved.

As a result of planning a book, by writing out bullet points on familiar subjects, a book will virtually write itself. It really starts to grow in the edit. One way to view a book, if you want to write one is to see it as an extension of a PowerPoint proposal. A PowerPoint proposal can easily be expanded to fill a book. Bullet points are like seeds, and they can grow as fast as your enthusiasm will permit.

The proposition behind this proposal is to share some ideas about how to start a business, with no money down, which is how all my businesses started. Unsurprisingly, people are interested in this subject. Sharing my experience results in this book being found. Some may want to work with you, some may buy more of your books, and some may refer to you or your books. It is both value sharing and a self-serving process. Everyone is a winner.

If there are no book sales and no new clients or any other kind of outcome, it matters little. If the book is a flop, no one will see it, nothing to be embarrassed about.

If your book is well received, then all good.

You will help some readers more than others. Should some of them have further interest, they can go online and get what they want at the books accompanying website. This approach is neat, as it avoids high-pressure sales tactics. It allows you to 'speak' openly by helping readers and, in turn, it may drum up interest from those who need further support.

It is simply impossible to please all the people all the time (ask any politician, although some are admittedly delusional.). Some will not enjoy openness, while others will decide whether your ideas are too simple for them. If your hand is on your heart and you genuinely try helping readers, then this will most likely work very well.

There is so much you can do. You can write a book, record a PowerPoint presentation, run a webinar, a podcast, set up a membership website, hand out free software, or document business processes. The creation of assets is very scalable, and most assets can be delivered as digital packages. This can help ensure your business goes viral (in a good way).

Be aware you do not just create assets from your imagination or research. Documenting systematic business processes is another way to create an asset. A system asset is one you use as well as potentially sell under license to others. Either as a blueprint a third party can follow or as an outsourced service where your team delivers a done for you service.

We are at an intriguing point. Many will decide, due to where they are at this moment, they can relate. Or we are in unfamiliar worlds, we communicate in a peculiar language, and we are based in unknown towns. The content is overly involved. This author is obviously a man. The reader is a woman, etc. It is easier for most of us to identify reasons to not act rather than to act. We all find it easy to cite differences, rather than similarities.

106

The better way to process events is to think further and to consider objections as challenges. You will get more from life if you think about how you can work in your world. With this line of thought, the chances are you can go much, much further.

If this is all too much information, then go through the ideas again. Pick out the items and prioritize a list. Decide to focus on the top three items that resonate with you the most. Get those done and then go back and reprioritize. It would be impossible for most of us to do all these things at once. It is absolutely possible to undertake and process a few of these ideas and execute them, one by one.

Many will state the suggestions are all well and good, yet they would not work in their market. Seizing an idea from one industry and making it work in another industry where it did not exist in the past is how millionaires are made. This is the essence of innovation. There are many references to the importance of innovation in business. It is not what you possess or what you appreciate, your future is all about how you make what you find work for your customers.

Sales

To succeed, we need to sell and acquire new customers to sell to.

As an entrepreneur, you absolutely must sell. Everyone sells. Yet most shy away from sales as salespeople have developed a dubious reputation for themselves and they are frequently depicted in films as being greedy. This is a great shame, as sales are all about making it easy for customers to purchase.

You will have sold to your parents or guardians on a balmy day when you wanted ice cream as a child. We all do it. A one-to-one presentation is a sales pitch, making the first impression as you walk through the door is about selling yourself. We all develop skills.

Broadly, the sales process is as simple as talking to people with a smile. The sales process does not always benefit from being overly persuasive. Frequently, you can sell the most by informing people what to do. Like: Do not launch a business until you have read this book. Just, for instance, you understand. Wink. If you want to practise persuasive techniques and get a little tricky, then read Persuasion by Robert Cialdini.

For me, the much-maligned NLP (Neuro-Linguistic Programming) is more relevant and useful. Again, the author's rendition of how it all works baffles, even after attending their controversial 'shows'. Instinctively, the NLP techniques are organic, not abnormally manipulative. Like all things though, you can have too much of a good thing and, in sales, you certainly become too pushy.

If you have a great offer, there is a lot less of a need to 'manipulate' or push for sales. I think the market is wise to high-pressure techniques anyway. If I am interested in a topic, high pressure approaches turn me off.

As one would expect, invariably, we cannot help ourselves from urging potential customers to buy now. In my case, the reason is genuinely my time availability. There is inevitably time and place.

Indeed, about time and place, you may remember the most compelling idea is to entice customers to come to you. When someone comes to you, they are a lot more likely to be predisposed to buy from you. They desire something you possess. They may appreciate you. Or, they know someone who has referred you. As a result, you do not need to be pushy or use hard sales techniques. The more you do, the more likely you will lose sales. When people come to you, they are telling you the time is right.

The ultimate sales technique

We are experts at what we do, yet the same avoidable mistakes keep occurring.

Many common critical disasters could be avoided. The good news is it is possible to get your message across, there is a simple process that works wonders, it is hidden in plain sight and should help to ensure fewer disasters occur going forward.

You must let it be known you have a solution to a problem and an initial consultation is available for free.

The offer of a free consultation is a win/win proposition, as occasionally an easy fix is found. At other times, a more detailed prescription is required, usually not a moment too soon. Easy fixes are good for PR, and these can help increase the volume of referrals. The more detailed prescription may lead to a big problem being solved as a result of services rendered.

Every professional offers a free consultation.

Why should you offer an initial free consultation?

Be it your doctor, lawyer, or Insurance Broker.

In the first meeting, the assessment of needs is usually free. You would seek a consultation knowing you had a problem to fix with an expert and the expert would provide you with further insights.

Insights discussed during an initial consultation could be enough to know whether the issue requires serious attention or if it would resolve of its own accord.

Usually, consultation is a delightful experience, offering relief.

You will typically benefit from the discovery of new methods to limit the problem or reduce its effects. The anticipated negative impact should be minimized, and the path ahead is defined to ensure it will remain free and clear.

Every case is different.

One-to-one consultations foster clear communication concentrated on the main areas of concern, highly personalized for the participants from the perspective of the wanted objectives and the consultants' area of expertise. A good consultation should result in an understanding by consulting whether the area of concern is an area of qualified domain experience, or not.

If not, then the outcome is usually that a referral is made to a consultant who has the relevant experience. However, referrals like this are exceptions and tend to occur in very technical cases. The majority of the time, the required experience is found as promised and remedies are discussed.

Personalization is key

If you are reviewing this from an advisory perspective, perhaps health or cybersecurity, the objective is to get your recipient to listen and take your advice.

The method identifies the objective and then discusses how the objectives may be best achieved while maintaining a strong health or cyber security posture.

From a sales perspective, by understanding the needs and objectives, you can see a tightly matching remedy that delivers on the core requirements and achieves the desired sale.

In both cases, all parties can be delighted and this is how advice is not only listened to but acted upon.

In many situations, a more detailed examination of the facts may be carried out to ensure all the angles are thoroughly investigated to ensure the proposed remedy is most likely to work. This is often followed up with a proposal, or detailed prescription.

The terms are noticeably interchangeable.

Further questions may arise, and changes or variations will be made to accommodate them. Some solutions may be automatic, some may be manual. Again, this is similar to health as it is for business applications.

Avoid the forced imperative

Mandated services are normally forced imperatives few welcome and less implement.

The consultative approach works especially well in mandated scenarios. If you avoid the consultation, you will likely face more problems and higher costs. As everyone is issued with an identical lump-it-or leave-it solution, which leads to reduced acceptance. It is then very hard to ensure compliance, especially if the only outcomes are force or failure.

In the commercial world, clients retain the opportunity to switch suppliers and often will without any hesitancy.

A good bedside manner instills good feelings

A good doctor, for example, may often be referred to as having a good bedside manner, which, of course, has no bearing on technical ability.

However, it has a lot of bearing on the results and trust delivered to patients. Better treatment may be an illusion. However, the service costs are likely to be lower and overall patient (client) satisfaction will be higher as a result.

The difference is simply one-to-one consultation.

It is for the same reasons some restaurants are perceived as being better when the food is often identical, the only difference is the one-to-one attention delivered by the waiter.

The waiter's prism

If we review the waiter's role through the prism of offering advice and having that advice acted upon, we can see why this can be an effective role and good for business, even though the waiter has nothing to do with the provision of food.

The waiter usually greets new guests at the door, representing the business, is impeccably turned out, and makes a welcome statement immediately followed by a question.

The question could be how can I help you or it may be what you are looking for today, or perhaps would you like me to escort you to a waiting table? Either way, it is a natural question and is easy to answer, dealing with the guests, and immediately the request is acted upon. The new guest is now personally escorted to a waiting table.

The waiter will then make further inquiries about their needs, and timing and potentially organize the table and some initial drinks, perhaps something as simple as locating and offering a water carafe. We are in full consultation mode where the waiter is serving the guest's needs, finding out how they can be helped, and actually helping them.

Visitors will soon be happy to order food from the menu and likely welcome suggestions from the waiter who knows the score and may make recommendations designed to ensure the comfort of the guests and to maximize the utility of the restaurant kitchens, leading to happy guests and a good income with the potential for return visits.

The benefit of the no-pressure pitch

There does not need to be pressure on anyone to buy anything at any time.

Guests arrive looking for service and it is provided, if it has faltered or if it is considered unsatisfactory, or if another venue has taken the guests' attention, they will move on.

If guests stay and take delivery of the service offered, then it is because it made total sense and felt right to them.

A quality consultation avoids manipulation

There is no hard sell or requirement to buy, as there is a win/win just from being of service.

Providing human and humane help is an excellent basis to build goodwill and, as a result, more will follow your advice.

More will recommend you and let others know you are the expert in the field they would recommend. With luck, the consultation experience may lend itself to building a reputational story where their experience of working with you is repeated.

This is the kind of story you want to have out there.

This is why this is the ultimate guide to ensure potential customers come to you, listen to what you have to say, and take action.

Next up: What to sell and when to sell it: you can expect to endure dark times before you see the sunlight of success. Do not cave into the unexpected pressures, when it comes to serving customers, there will however be some fine tuning to do. You will get to determine your start-up type, and this will give you insights into how to position your business and what to look for in potential customers.

The next chapter will help you to steer a course away from the rocks of doom and disaster. This is precisely why you should know where those rocks lie and have more ideas about how to avoid even more pitfalls.

In chapter 6: What to sell and when to sell it, you will also discover:

- How focus can maximize your sales opportunities.
- **The almost magical match between start-up type and target market group.**
- How to create custom assets to demonstrate your very tight market match.
- **Systemize your business and sell licenses for quick cash and rolling income.**
- How to get to know who your top 20% target customers really are.
- **What can you outsource to ensure you have a passive income?**

Chapter 6:

What to sell and when to sell it

It is critical to concentrate on the needs of customers and what they want to purchase.

You will not gain the requisite knowledge and ideas to aid you solve challenges and move forward if you do not do so. Even if you have plenty of time and resources, terrible initial decisions have sunk many start-ups.

The first internet sensation: webvan.com raised hundreds of millions and had a valuation in the billions. However, it had placed market commitments to the tens of billions, written many man-years of software and hired thousands of staff. This was all before they realized they never did have the customers they expected. The business was unsustainable as they did not possess the customers they needed to maintain costs. Webvan had made the fatal mistake of implementing the vision without knowing if customers would follow through.

However, if you execute an unfortunate no money decision, you can quickly reverse it. Webvan had $178.5 million in revenue and over $525 million in costs at its peak in 2000. They had chosen to concentrate on their vision and its implementation rather than customer needs and desires. Hence the enormous mismatch. At the end, the business had billions of expenses committed too. The lack of customers turned out to represent their most critical issue.

Lack of customers and poor sales revenues is the Achilles heel of just about every start-up. Everyone faces the same problem. Despite this, many start-ups ignore customers, particularly if someone else provides the cash to run the business in the short term and the technology shows promise and looks hot and sexy.

Focusing on fixing customer requirements before they become an issue is the best way to entice customers and avoid epic failure and bankruptcy. Figure out what customers require, and then decide whether to design it to their specifications. You determine what to produce, when to produce it, and whether you will deliver it. You should expect to test what a potential customer says they want, as often what they say they want and what they should have, or need are different things.

You will want to keep shipping costs down and make delivery as easy and quick as possible. Over time, you can add complexity, breadth, and refinement. Only make sure your innovative solutions are in line with known customer requirements. The proof will always be in advance orders from paying customers.

My first 'proper' business was selling specialist computer keyboards. Designed to my unique specification, they were to be made in a new German factory. At only 21, green and wet behind the ears, with no money, no experience, the minimum order was fifty thousand pieces.

Booked orders at the time: five. I had orders and prepayments. These were customers. Liability was never a consideration. Fortunately, they came in batches making them easier to sell and handle. Two years later all fifty thousand units had been sold.

A few weeks after starting, my mum got the details. She was so shocked she screamed I would be taken to prison! It was a memorable moment. Not the right way to run a business without any money. The business world was a lot more trusting back then.

The most troublesome part was when Herr Schmidt wanted to descend on my office. Which was the local pub. No office, no car, no staff. There were no taxis convenient to collect the promised entourage from Heathrow on the day either. However, it was possible to hire a limousine.

The night before one of my friends came into the pub and asked if any of us would be 'free' tomorrow. Reluctantly I said, 'looks like I will be' to which he stated "great, you can help me clear my dad's office". An extremely appealing idea occurred to me.

Where is your dad's office? Is it vacant now? Can I borrow it tomorrow lunchtime? The B.A.T. Building. 22nd floor. Yes. Wow, it was the most glamorous, tallest building in town and now I possessed the keys!

Imagine it. The German entourage was collected from Heathrow by a big, long black stretch limo with little old me in inside. We drove into town seemingly like royalty. We must have been quite the sight as we were deposited at the fabulous front entrance of the B.A.T. building which seems to sweep you into the foyer. We hastily (collected our cleaners' badges and) packed into the lift to the 22nd floor. We took in the views (for the first time in my life) and we talked.

Clearly the chief thing the Germans wanted was a signed order. The focus was on the development costs set at thousands of Deutschmarks (this was before the Euro). My dominant thought to this point had always been who would buy the next pint? My concept of negotiation was non-existent. The sum suggested to cover R&D was merely an accepted fantastical number. Ultimately, it occurred to me to pay it all at the rate of 5 'marks per keyboard.

The German entourage were delighted. They jumped to their feet, shook my hand, and shoved the paperwork across the desk. I signed. Somehow the group of Germans disappeared. Herr Schmidt was never seen again.

Now a commitment to accept delivery of fifty thousand keyboards existed. Not the best outcome I could have hoped for, although I was completely naïve and unaware of the financial risk. Ignorance is bliss!

I was still living with my parents when the first batch of five hundred keyboards arrived outside my house. The huge, multi-part, articulated lorry blocked out the sun. It was subsequently discovered the keyboards did not work... They did get fixed, after two weeks without sleep. A story I can summarize in one word: endurance!

The point is things go wrong. You cannot predict when or how. You just find a way and keep moving forward. Even in the face of insurmountable odds and danger. Indeed, even when you do not have the money and seemingly no way to pay what you owe.

It helps to start with a rabid customer base and a great product. I knew there were fanatical hobbyist customers. I felt the keyboard would be great. Luckily, everybody worshipped it on sight. The keyboards were beautiful, and they sold like hot cakes.

Larger than life sized posters were produced so retailers could demonstrate the keyboard in their shops without taking stock, useful as I did not have much stock to start with. This drove orders and caused customers to send money.

It was not really until the last of the keyboards was sold when I could finally breathe properly again. Two years zipped along as those keyboards were pushed out. It was an incredibly fortunate escape for all the obvious reasons.

The profits paid for my youth and my first house too. The good news is as a considerably older man there is no need for me to go buy a flash sports car - having possessed one in my twenties!

My low slung, super cool, high-speed car was sent tobogganing across a French field at one point. The roads and fields on the way home from Paris were covered in icy snow. The passenger and driver are incredibly lucky to be alive all things considered. Plus, it turned out we were not insured properly either, so my super car got paid for twice over.

It was because of looking for and then nurturing customers I was able to quickly get over and recover from the various 'accidents' which beset me. Most were those created, in my naivety, for myself. I became a quick learner and gradually 'accidents' reduced.

As you become more experienced, more practiced in business, you become more aware of the pitfalls, and they happen less often. However, there was one phrase I heard too many times, although it still bears repeating - 'ah well, you are young enough to recover'.

Indeed, as time has progressed, a more straightforward business is preferred.

Currently, there is just one member of staff (me). No car, no office, and a single bank account with everything cut to the bone. There is no ostentation, no foyer, no waiting area, no potted plants. No car plan or C Suite. Just me, a PC, and a mobile phone. Much less to go wrong, cause delay or get in the way of things. Plus, money comes in through a range of independent, passive income sources. Accounting fees are lower, taxation, health and safety simplified, overheads almost zero.

Having a great product for fanatical customers with good enough marketing made the keyboard business work well. It was possible to deliver to customers exactly what they demanded. So many were desperate for a better keyboard than the one provided with the horrible rubber keyed Sinclair ZX Spectrum.

All we needed to offer was a picture of what they could have. The stock would sell as promptly as it arrived. I had to have much delivered by air. At times Germany could not produce keyboards fast enough.

3 businesses with no cash down

If you have no cash, no customers, and no time, what can you do? Publishing a guide or book on Amazon is an example of something you can do extremely rapidly and inexpensively. You decide what to write, you decide what the cover looks like, and you decide on the price to charge for the whole package. An entirely passive, set and forget business.

If you do not want to write you can hire a ghost writer via upwork.com.

If you are not a designer, you can get a book cover designed on fiverr.com. You do not have to sell your book either, just upload it to Amazon.

If you do not fancy publishing, you could recruit agents to run a business for you. You pay agents a percentage of sales. This makes you their joint venture partner and secures them to the business. This can work effectively, especially if you are prepared to furnish them with more information, systems, and processes over time.

License agreements can deliver even more. In the U.K. licensing is better known as franchising. Potentially you could earn a percentage from every sale without you having to give up any time or money to service or find customers.

You should retain the copyright on the information you write and supply to those agents. The business ideas will remain your intellectual property.

No money down, no staff to hire, and potentially an unlimited income stream with no customers to manage either! Everything and anything is possible with licensing and copyright protection.

If the business is based on your experience, it can take little time to assemble as you presumably already possess all you require.

There are many businesses you can build up and manage like this.

For instance, almost any specialist consulting business, legal practice, or an R&D tax reduction business. You can run the business, organize the sales and when it grows outsource to partners, agents, or licensees.

Practically any industry with specialist staff can operate this way. It is routine for recruitment specialists to put consultancy groups together. This is typical in specialist areas of electronics, cybersecurity, nursing, and so on.

There are many ways to secure new customers.

A lead-generating book, a video series, podcast series, social media posts, email campaigns, referral campaigns, well placed problem-solution articles and so on.

Nowadays you can forward all enquiries instantly, automatically, without lifting a finger, merely by supplying a link. Your partners will grant you a commission. Online this is recognized as affiliate marketing. Millions are generated this way.

There are many business opportunities which require no cash down, based on passive and active income strategies by doing or managing the work and outsourcing, partnering, or licensing.

What type of business will you start?

When it comes to starting up in business, a business will tend to find itself in one of four categories.

Knowing your category is critical. My biggest successes have been in completely new areas, although they were found within existing known markets.

In the past I would see an opportunity and make it my own. I started many different businesses. Here are three example multi-million business I started:

I established a substantial keyboard business because the Sinclair ZX Spectrum had a poor keyboard. The keyboard was universally panned as it was obviously cheap, rectangular, a rubber membrane, not particularly tactile. My solution was beautiful, it hid the Sinclair ZX Spectrum and had full travel, professional looking individual, tactile keys.

A few years later I established a business to support financial services firms. I decided it was a good idea to focus on markets that had the money.

I went on to establish a services business in the search engine marketing sector when I pioneered the search marketing agency Weboptimiser in the 1990's. It was possible to be listed within many search engines for free if you could alter the code of your website and let the search engines know your website existed. All good until nearly twenty years later, following the invention of pay per click and now there is primarily only google.

The 4 start-up types of businesses

Each type of business requires a different perspective to succeed.

The perspective required can largely be determined by classifying your business type.

The main business types:

1. You serve an existing market.
2. You serve an entirely new market.
3. You serve an existing market with low prices.
4. You serve an existing market with a new niche offer.

#1 The most successful challenge to the status quo is to disrupt an existing market.

However, you may have to face established competition, who already know who the customers in the market are. They may have already secured long-term supply arrangements, ensuring new entrants are 'locked out'. This is not impossible, although you will need to think about your competitive difference beyond type #3, price.

#2 Serving an entirely new market is possibly the hardest to be successful.

There is a reason why pioneers are said to have arrows in their backs. This enterprise will most likely require a lot of capital. You will want to find a way to discretely test the market and find a way to enter it without needing a lot of money to do so and without alerting potential competitors of the existence of the opportunity. Can be difficult to achieve success. Although licensing may be a stealth approach and would secure long-term supply arrangements.

Serving an entirely new market is to be avoided unless you are starting with a unique or special location or have protective attributes such as patents or copyright in place.

#3 If you compete on price, chances are high you will sacrifice profit.

Market incumbents may have built up a war chest or have access to capital. They may have the deals they need in place to survive, all they need to do is to change their price to compete on price. Although there may be other values in play you may not appreciate. Competitors may differentiate their product beyond price, and this may show you up.

Chances are if you compete on price, you may well compromise profitability and margin too. This can be a difficult market position to be in, particularly if you wish to raise capital at some point in the future. While some companies have lasted for decades, the focus is on slowing the race to the bottom. Starting at the bottom, does not help the cause. Lower margins will count against you. You may have to reduce prices and margins further unless you employ an 80:20 top slicing, premium customer attracting strategy.

#4 A winning approach is to change the game by extending the market opportunities of an existing customer base.

Thus, you can let others pioneer, while you offer solutions to address specific, known needs. This would allow you to carve out an area of specialization and potentially command premium rates without having to spend prodigious amounts on marketing. However, you will forever be reliant on the market host. There would generally be nothing to stop the host from competing with you, although the host may have bigger fish to fry, and potentially remain ignorant.

#1 and #4 are my favorites. Market disruption has proven to be very lucrative for many in dot-com businesses. #4 can be long lasting, although I have found when the host moves on or changes the game, you can suddenly find yourself out of business, so it can be precarious. However, not everyone can come up with a total game changer. Sometimes what starts as a game changer may develop and become an additional add-on.

David Whites' Start-up Rule #6
Know what kind of start-up you are

What to sell and when to sell it

When you focus on the needs of customers you will tend to establish what they want to buy.

Based on customer interests it is best to work out what you can deliver quickly and fast. This way if it is not accepted it may lead to discussion and revision. If a customer accepts your initial offer, then congratulations you have found a customer. You should now focus on delivering quickly and efficiently. This is the key to the establishment of a start-up.

When you have established a start-up based on actual customer needs you can attempt to work out the type of business you are in #1 to #4. This information will help you to understand the best approach to moving forward with the marketing and coordination of the business.

You will often find a customer will want something slightly different to what you offer. In many cases customers prefer solutions tailored to their needs. This is great, as this can lead you to being the only person capable of making the delivery and therefore the only supplier. This will help to ensure further business opportunity, customers will return to become clients.

There are business opportunities you could focus on for rapid results. The first is almost certainly to offer advisory or consultancy services. Publishing can involve no one else and can cost almost nothing, especially if you already have the content you need to hand. Next, you can take a little bit of time to recruit agents.

Ideally agents are already in the field.

Sometimes agents are known as brokers and are common in many industries. You dictate the terms of business and your agents operate the system you provide. The agents may be paid fees and a commission on sales. Next, is to license a business process you have perfected directly. In time, there is no reason why you cannot employ all these techniques to maximize your income.

Speed is of the essence, the sooner you take an order, the sooner you get paid. It is up to you to decide your terms of business. Large companies dealing with other large companies may take a lifetime to pay, however, most large companies recognize a small amount paid upfront to a small supplier can be enormously helpful and often, they like to do it, so ask.

Although you probably have all you need, see if you can assemble a team of people to supply to your customer, chances are you will get paid more for this too. However, you do need to be very tight on your terms with your team and with the customer. You may have to insist on a deposit or upfront payment or payment with order to cover the costs of labor.

Writing is an imperative skill. It is difficult to run a business without writing, so go all in and write a book or two. People will see your commitment and dedication otherwise, plus we all like an author. Books are still treated by millions with reverence, and you will stand out from your competitors and the distribution and sales of your non-fiction 'how-to' book will drive a small income and more potential customers direct to you too.

When creating content start by defining a set of bullet points, try recording a video of you reading through them. Discuss the bullet points and record it on your mobile phone video and upload it to YouTube privately, to extract the transcript text file, which is free and fast. You can use the transcript as the basis for the first draft of your book which will save you thinking and writing time. It could give you a head start and if done well could provide a set of media resources for you ready to use without any major investment.

You can take advantage of services like Amazon KDP to publish and print brochures, guides, and books. You can expect a total cost of about five dollars for a book of this type on a DIY basis. Delivery will take about a week, sometimes next day.

Writing, recording, producing books is all about the creation of assets. These can be valued and appear itemized as intellectual property on your balance sheet.

Constantly creating, talking, tinkering, staying in the flow, is enjoyable. Helping new customers to become clients is the most enjoyable part. You will find more on this important topic in the following chapter.

Next up: Convert customers to clients. Discover the first thing to look for when looking at a potential business opportunity and the value of converting customers to clients.

Don't miss this next chapter as it will help you with the key insights to make sure you maximize your customer relationships, so they keep paying out for the longest possible time.

In chapter 7: Convert customers to clients, you will also discover:

- How to convert customers to clients to ensure your income grows and grows.
- **How your tailor can provide insights into cultivating professionalism**
- How to use the 80:20 rule to pull out the most lucrative clients
- **Learn the best way to manage difficult, loss-making clients.**
- Outsource cash and credit management if you want to sleep better at night.
- **Thoughts on the ideal business and how to keep costs low.**

Chapter 7:

Convert customers to clients

The first thing I like to look for in a business opportunity is what I like to call the 'milk round'. The term 'milk-round' comes from the days when milk was delivered door to door. Every day the milkman would set out to do his milk deliveries. The milkman knew who wanted what, where. The milkman literally had a round of paying customers.

In my opinion, ongoing, paying customers are better referred to as clients. I prefer the word clients; these are upgraded customers. You need to find a customer first; you need to find a customer by making a sale. You find a client by developing the relationship by selling a personalized service tuned exactly to their needs and supplying them on an ongoing, regular basis.

Clients usually prefer it. You can give clients special discounts or service quality upgrades in return for signing up. It can be very worthwhile for all involved if you could find premium clients and deliver a premium service too. Clients are a win/win. Clients know they get preferred treatment this way too.

Clients should always know they will be first in line and get higher levels of service. In return, you get ongoing, calculable, dependable, regular, and repeat business from people you like. Your business can rely on a more stable, expected income pipeline with a sustainable margin. In fact, the price with clients often becomes irrelevant.

Clients want to do business with you, and they are often prepared to pay more for the privilege. The passage of moving from simply finding and servicing customers to clients is a sign of business potential. As a business owner, moving customers to clients is very reassuring, it tells you, you are doing a lot right.

All sorts of financial services open when you can show a bank you have regular contracted clients. This is what financial executives and accountants may refer to as your 'book'. Business valuations are determined by the size of your book. If you try to sell a business in the future, due diligence will look for evidence of who is in your book.

Specialist, due diligence accountants use specific formulas to determine the value of your business based on your book. Their objective is to show the split between ongoing and new revenue. From this, they will try to estimate the future value of the business. This helps them to put value on your business.

However, an actual long-term investor will look for a minimum period too. An investor would look for an ongoing history of years not months. Usually, three years is the minimum. Your first client, nevertheless, should provide you with a certain amount of pride and knowledge of what could be to come.

There is nothing better than knowing who your clients are. The difference between customers and clients is that you know more about them. You have a relationship with them, and they know you by name too. These are based on a developed friendship, usually because of appreciation of your skill or craftsmanship or simply good social skills. Good customer service and client appreciation can help too. It can be as simple as being nice to people. Strong relationships are often valued more than service delivery.

Considering customers as clients can be a genuine differentiator, producing a powerful effect on your bank account too.

Probably, the most important thing to understand is that developing clients from customers can be done at zero to no cost at all. It is all achieved based on what you say and how you do what you do.

David Whites' Start-up Rule #7
Clients can cost nothing to cultivate.

The professional tailor

Your tailor will talk to you while measuring your height, arm length, inside legs, etc. Your tailor will take notes and suggest color and materials to suit. Very quickly, your tailor will discover what you like and what works and have enough information to make sure everything will fit you perfectly. It is genuinely a delightful experience.

Most of us will be prepared to pay whatever the tailor suggests. We tend to enjoy the tailored finish a tailor can provide. Chances are, as well as agreeably paying over the top, we will go back and pay top dollar again and again.

Building your milk-round

As a teenager, on sunny Saturdays with friend, we would knock on the doors of nearby neighbors. We would ask if the householder wanted their car to be washed. Few were rude, many simply said no thanks, a few said yes please and yet others said yes and congratulated our initiative. Afterall, most car owners have kids and most like to reward those who work for them.

The next week, we knew whose door to knock on. We also knocked on the other doors again. This time, some of the folk, some of those who had first said no, now said yes. They recognized us, and we recognized them. I learned the power of building a round and not taking no for an answer.

Car cleaning was back-breaking work, although some of those cars were supercars! We would clean 5-10 cars a day, we would end up with 20 to 30 bucks each and, as teenagers, this was big, easy money. Naturally, we would celebrate with cider. We also saved some of the cash and later we bought our own motorbikes and then, later, cars.

In my late twenties, after a successful keyboard business, I found myself on the wrong side of cash. Needing to boost my income. Knowing the principles, I was able to build another business. I came up with the idea of selling computer networks.

It was at the start of the PC 'revolution' and all businesses wanted their own PC's. I had experience already. I knew where to get the parts from, and I knew how to get them to work. I sold a few. It was slow, although the money was great, clients had to pay me upfront. Not all were willing. Eventually, credit terms were negotiated, and this became easier. In the early days of business, cash was the only option, cash was king.

Businesses wear uniforms

I saw another opportunity, to sell sandwiches and snacks on a nearby trading estate. It was a money-generating business and at the time I needed cash, and I was prepared to work. I wore a suit to sell computer networks and a T-shirt and jeans when selling snacks and sandwiches.

One day, a network customer was in the queue. He did not flinch, he bought a sandwich, crisps, and a coke. He did not say a word. We recognized each other for sure. We never discussed it, and in the afternoons the sale of networks continued.

Sandwich sales quickly ceased. The computer networks were bigger. Strong relationships and entrepreneurial respect saved the day.

However, I was not going to take the risk anymore just for a few extra bucks. I needed to adjust upwards and could not lapse. I realized I had to look the part and vowed I would only appear again wearing a suit. I counted out the possibility of selling sandwiches and snacks!

Top Slicing

Many have the business idea of selling at the lowest price. With this kind of business attitude, it is difficult to continue if the market shifts down, as you are left with nowhere to go. It becomes, as they say, a race to the bottom. If this is your game, at some point, your margins will collapse to zero or less. At this point, you will lose the business. Possibly your shirt too. Inevitably, this is exactly what happens time and time again.

Yet if you look at your sales numbers, if you are in a price-sensitive niche, you will find some customers buy more. Some by volume, some by value. Some always only buy premium, more expensive lines. These are the customers you want to focus on. They are more lucrative, where time and effort will most likely be rewarded. These are the most likely to convert to becoming clients.

You will want to learn why these customers spend what they spend and what they use your product or service for. This information may help you find more ways to help them and sell even more. This type of customer exists in most businesses.

You may have heard about the Pareto Principle. The Pareto Principle exists in nature as well as being consistent in business. 20 percent of plants grow 80 percent of the produce. In business, as a rule, 20 percent of your clients will bring 80 percent of your profits.

If you are new to a business, the Pareto Principle may be a big revelation. If you are experienced in business, you may know this. Either way, use this information to your advantage by organizing your business around the top 20 percent as it will keep you going when times are hard.

A classic new business strategy

The 80:20 rule can be employed to win new business using a loss-leader approach to find more clients. When you know who is interested, you can focus on those to filter and find bigger players. This is a well-worn, tried, and tested method for growing a business that many deploy subconsciously.

The loss leader is an exercise where you make an offer where you do not expect to make a lot of money, or any profit, perhaps even a loss. However, when someone takes advantage of your offer, the chances are, they will become a good prospect for your business.

The common alternative to this is the gift. Where gifts are provided to customers for free. It may cost you some money, online this is usually furnished by way of information. You can also promote reusable assets for this purpose. A downloadable PDF, for instance, in exchange for an email address.

For example, there is an offer on my website:

https://TheAuthorityFigure.com/

You can download my Start-up Rules PDF and you can get access to my free discussion videos and how you can apply these ideas to your business development and answer your questions. The site adds value to this book, which also enables the development of customers to clients.

These promotional ideas are referred to as lead magnets and may take the form of a coupon, discount, free resources, or e-book. The main method is to help visitors, or readers in this case, to achieve their objectives.

My example offers more focus on how to start a new business without any money and I will answer questions too. Most fail to make strong enough offers, or any offer. A strong offer needs to tie in. In this case, the offer is made in the context of this book, and if you have read this far, then as a reader, the chances are you are genuinely interested in the topic. You should find the resources available at the website of great interest.

This is not to say you must not spend any money, of course. You can, the point of this book, is you have a choice.

The more you get to know about your customer, the more you tailor your offering to suit them, the more customers convert to becoming clients. The more you will be able to talk to them by name and the more they will know your name and prefer to do business with you. Often, they will pay more. Plus, when you offer additional options and alternatives, the chances are increased they will buy from you, and you, alone.

If you can help your clients feel proud and honored to work with you, the more likely they will refer to you and refer you to others too.

You can reasonably charge clients higher prices. After all, you will be providing a personalized service. This is the difference clients can mean to a business. You become their preferred supplier. Being a preferred supplier means you have earned your clients' trust to always deliver the goods. They will often tell you things to help your business too, including what they think they will want in the future and even place future orders on you.

I learned early on when I was cleaning cars. I started to use a little black book. As clients would tell me certain things, such as how often to return. What specifically to clean or take special care over. Or what it was they wanted to polish or for us to be careful of. Everything went into my little black book. Clients were delighted when I 'remembered'.

Clients like to see you taking the time to care. After a while, clients gave their phone numbers for convenience. Rather than turn up randomly, we would set appointments and turn up at a given time as agreed. In this way, we would get the work we wanted, and they would get the car cleaned when it was convenient for them. This increased client satisfaction and ensured we got the most money from the time spent working on most cars.

Later, when running the first digital marketing agency in the 90s and beyond, we did the same thing, it was all about timing. We would have regular clients, our 'round'. We would hold regular monthly meetings with each other. We would discuss and report the months' activities and look out for specific areas of interest, current or new promotions and so it continued almost perpetually for more than a decade.

Problem client management

Another key issue when looking for customers to turn into clients is to make sure you like them. It took me a long time to learn this lesson. This lesson is hard for many new to business. Take on only the clients you like. The tendency is to take on all clients, as they all pay money. Money is the point, right? I learned for some clients. Money is never enough.

I have met some genuinely nice people who make a habit of shouting at and being rude to suppliers. Simply because they are boss, and they are paying for service. Come hell or high water, they are going to get it. Whether you give it to them or not. These are the ones where it does not matter how hard or well you work. They always find problems. It turns out that their main expertise is to turn molehills into mountains.

For my first few years in business (in reality, an exceptionally long time) I honestly believed the phrase: 'the customer is always right'. Unfortunately, it is not true. This wrong belief really stumped my initial growth. As politicians certainly know. It is impossible to please all the people all the time. Yet for some reason. We all set out to keep everyone happy. Is it really the right thing to do? I still want clients to be happy, but only if it is possible for them and I to be happy. It seems that some are simply impossible to please.

Problem clients can be subtle. For example, a service client would accept the delivery as good, the invoice was issued, and we would automatically roll into the next month of service. This meant we would continue to allocate manpower, which meant wages and overhead costs to manage the delivery.

Out of the blue, we would receive a request to pop over to the client's office, which would occur a few days later, as arranged. We would be told how delighted the clients were. How well things were going. There was, however, a small issue concerning them that they would ask us to rectify. We would review and agree to rectify the issue. We would resolve it and expect payment. It would usually be something minor, an easy fix.

When payment did not arrive, we would call and be invited back. Sure enough, a few days later we would meet up. The client would explain that the invoice had been passed for payment. Yet, due to the issue, the invoice was not processed last month, and only since the issue was rectified has it been passed for payment now. It will be paid at the end of the current month. Of course, we needed cash, our margins were tight, and we had wages due. The manager or business owner may see his or her way to advance us. This would be considered a big favor, considering it was all caused because of our delinquency in the delivery of the contract in the first place. It appears reasonable.

You would imagine correctly, when you have clients like these, this affects cash flow and profitability. You could say it was our fault for under-delivery, yet this problem does not manifest with other clients. We could easily find ourselves in the hole for three months' worth of costs. This is nearly a year's worth of profits for this type of business. We were eventually forced to conclude that those types of clients were not worth the ongoing risk of eventual non-payment and terminal dispute.

Reluctantly, we realized the inevitable. Certain clients had to go. We could not afford months of low payments. We would inform the client that we would have to hang fire on service for a month. As, naturally, we could not afford to pay staff wages until we had the cash to pay them.

I would discuss this face-to-face and not tell the client it was their fault or try to blame the client or ask anything from the client. It would simply be presented as an apologetic, no-fault fact. We cannot continue, we need time to regroup, perhaps there is another supplier who could help them, we have had to let staff go. They would not like the suggestion, although we still had hope for the future, it would appear we were on our knees and there was no alternative.

We would eventually be paid. We would then simply inform the client that we did not think we had any services we could sell them. The delayed payments and our small margins meant that the business between us did not work. Not a single client in this position offered to pay more. Paying less, paying slowly, or not paying at all was their game all along.

The imposition of credit limits

It was as a result of slow-players and worse (clients who never paid) I learned to understand how to use credit limits and credit scoring through factoring. This meant that our business would sell invoices to the bank for a small percentage. The bank would vet clients, set credit limits, chase the money, and pay us the advances we needed. This also meant that the invoices were insured, so if there was bad debt, everything would be good.

Funnily enough, when sales were controlled in this way, debts and unpaid clients evaporated.

It also meant we did not waste time trying to appease weasel clients. Some just are, and they are difficult to spot and unless you deal with them, they keep on turning up. Sometimes clients do not mean to be mean. Misunderstandings can occur and are generally easy to resolve.

Unsurprisingly, when there is a bank involved, financial issues tend to get sorted quickly. If clients end up owing the money to a bank, they are more likely to pay. As not paying a major bank could lead to a bad credit rating for them.

For what we paid in percentages and fees, plus the time saved, it was more than worthwhile. We collected a lot more than the cost. We estimated the annual cost of several million in turnover equated to the cost of just one extra bookkeeper, a bargain.

The extra peace of mind was life-changing. When needed, the bank would issue cash advances from time to time too. This meant holidays or events could be attended without having to worry all day about cash flow.

An ideal business

An ideal business is no overhead, no people, no clients. Indeed, passive-income businesses is ideal.

In these times, this is achieved through the focus on the creation of finished assets.

For example, composing a book and publishing it on Amazon is passive. Amazon handles everything. Clients obtain everything they desire, including a refund with a smile, the Amazon smile. Nothing to do with me whatsoever. However, if a customer presents him or herself to me, they tend to arrive with a smile. They tend to have already decided to play nice, and this is how we all get along. It is tremendous, a significant win, win!

To use the milk round analogy, Amazon builds the round for me. Amazon handles the books, processes the payments, and keeps a decent chunk of the sales for their efforts.

Some of the readers filter through to me, they would be the top 20%. Are you one of the top 20%? Want to get involved? Visit the books accompanying website:

https://TheAuthorityFigure.com/

There are many following this route, so there is no need for the hard sell.

Next up: Massive opportunities for service businesses. If you are still wondering about how you manage time and money and find lucrative clients, the next chapter should provide many insights.

In chapter 8: Massive opportunities for service businesses, you will discover:

- How to apply the agile process to your business.

How To WoW!!

Chapter 8:

Massive opportunities for service business

Before the pandemic service sectors in both the UK and US had been on the up and up at reasonably high rates of growth year on year. There are many reasons for this.

Service businesses are principally those not involved in the extraction or manufacture of raw materials. In recent years, massive changes have occurred due to the introduction of an increase attributed to outsourcing, automation and digital-based businesses. In many cases, this has altered the way business is conducted and the connected business models for income.

Already diverse, the service industry is well established in consulting, accounting, and legal sectors. In addition, there are the advertising, marketing, and training sectors.

There was an increasing demand for diverse health, education, and entertainment services. The pandemic caused a general contraction in those areas with health excluding much else apart from covid out of necessity.

Digital markets have generally been disrupted during the last two decades. The focus has increased during the pandemic as some of the few rising stars are those who traded online rather than exclusively through retail establishments. The key opportunity in digital is where suppliers realize location does not limit their business opportunities. The market has got used to the idea that working remotely does not just work, it is safer and preferred by many.

The digital economy has been particularly disruptive when considered in the context of the gig economy, In an area like local transport. Customer suppliers and route management are easily coordinated digitally, much to the chagrin of traditional taxi operators. Other sectors, like the hotel industry, have been disrupted due to the creation of Air BnB. It has become more straightforward to hire out our spare rooms and drive our own cars for many to find additional income opportunities.

One by one, this has allowed smaller businesses to become more sophisticated in their service delivery. Increasingly, there are more opportunities for them to outsource customer service requirements. Instead of undertaking the work directly, we manage more of the work. This has led to more specialization and larger case loads, leading to more applied expertise. In turn, this delivers more consistent, higher-quality production where everyone is a winner.

When you manage a private firm or practice, money is tight as there is not much of it about, especially in start-up mode. For the city, a start-up is generally too small to have any commercial value unless there is a link of significance or until constant sales achieve a certain level. If your start-up reaches a certain threshold, changes can occur rapidly.

There are, however, various stock markets where the difference between them tends to represent the capitalization of those markets, i.e., relatively substantial money and unlimited money availability. For many business owners, getting listed on any stock market represents an exceptional achievement.

The junior markets are considered stepping-stones to get eventual access to more sizeable markets. Being listed in any market means you believe your enterprise is likely to deliver sustainable upward growth. Businesses require access to finance to facilitate growth and this is one benefit a business would achieve through a market listing.

For listed businesses, cash is the objective and often an issue. They potentially have access to unlimited levels of funding, yet more important to them is time and results. In the time they possess, they must make certain they continue to cultivate and demonstrate growth, especially in sales. Therefore, the services market can be extremely lucrative. There are many opportunities to work with businesses, which provide cash. Your private business can supply time and may be nimble enough to facilitate the results they require.

David Whites' Start-up Rule #8
Target customers who are
<u>cash rich, time poor</u>

The agile business process

When you consider the process of iteration from a project management perspective, you learn the agile system relies on private teams working independently. Stakeholders provide guidance, where the guidance may be to set boundaries. The source of information to facilitate cross-team co-operation is invariably also defined.

The agile manifesto favors individuals and interactions over processes and tools. Working software over comprehensive documentation. Customer collaboration over contract negotiation and responding to change over following a plan. These tenants were originally agreed upon and defined in the late 80s. It has required a few decades to prove not only are these the best and correct assertions, but these same ideas work beyond the confines of software development. Indeed, they work in every field.

Agile is a project management system. You could start anywhere, for instance: at either end, work forward or backward, or if it is appropriate, you could start in a central position and work outward in both directions.

The normal alternative is the waterfall project management system where you would not start in the middle or the end. You should always start from the beginning. For instance, if you were in construction, you would always start with a hole in the ground as opposed to mid-air.

You may employ an agile project management strategy for certain parts, fit out, for instance, but rarely build. However, the methodologies can, as suggested, be mixed. You may be familiar with them.

One method does not necessarily replace the other.

Agile and Lean lend themselves to where we know we want to innovate. We just do not know yet what we might innovate. Whereas the waterfall methodology of project management lends itself to situations where beginning-to-end elements generally follow an accepted pattern or order.

Interestingly, if we look at innovation from the two perspectives of waterfall and agile, we discover waterfall processes tend to be focused on precise and specific features. These can cause the price and time to vary, both of which are broadly of considerable concern to business managers. While agile is focused on providing what we can in the time and for the money we have, with the variable being features.

This difference in focus steers us to produce minimum viable products (MVPs). These support us in getting closer to delivering hope and verification through demonstrations.

If we are focused on features, then the determination for success comprises all the elements we want to be made available. A process of Iterative Innovation TM (Trademark Registered by me) means we can focus on the features we want to demonstrate first. If features are designed to be proven by demonstration, then we can go some way toward user acceptance testing.

Without user acceptance testing, it could be possible for what the clients desire and what the designers construct to remain miles apart. You may start discovering the attraction of agile. With an agile approach, we may possess an extensive list of features we like. Knowing, we want to witness the results. We determine the results we require. The first outcome we would consider valuable should demonstrate real customer benefits. Straight away, we can focus on value.

By eliminating for now all other features, we can focus on key delivery. Our chances of delivery for a minimum cost in a minimum time frame are considerably higher.

Apply the agile process to your business.

To apply the agile process to a start-up business, the first thing we require is a customer. Where a customer is a key feature. We do not worry about aesthetics. They come later when we know what the customer is considering.

If we looked at a start-up from the waterfall perspective, we would have to ensure everything was in place first before we could open for business. Imagine the cost implications and delays.

These two methods underline why the first focus must be on getting the customer first. Connect the bells and whistles if you desire and require them, later when you have received the money to invest in them.

Once we have completed the first round of development and iteration, we can choose to accept what we have and move forward. In the same way, once we have won our primary client, we can move forward as now we recognize what a customer might desire from us for sure.

We can modify our approach to achieve improvements. Or we can abandon the project as we have proven we cannot achieve the minimum. Or we can choose to delay the process, to allocate more time to fixing problems we can now foresee, those which we could not envision before.

Most importantly, having sight of results, even and including disappointing results or unexpected problems, provides management a choice. Business managers can decide whether to abandon or continue, how and when to allocate further time or money. The reasons can be independent of the project itself. It may simply be prudent due to economic, business, or market circumstances to delay development.

The point remains that a business can and should have all this under control.

In addition, with a reliable result, the business may find itself with a prototype. Experimental developments may be demonstrated to investors and may be spun off early in life based on the future potential of the project.

To a great degree, the process of iteration is extremely business-management-friendly. It is tremendous to be a part of the delivery team as it is frequently challenging to obtain success even when the objectives are simplified and reduced.

Iteration has another powerful motivation built-in, and it specifically outlaws: scope creep. By targeting specific features, none more can be added until the minimum agreed features are delivered.

We can conceive more markedly brilliant ideas. We can manage them according to a coherent system known as MoSCoW rules: must have, should have, could have, and will not have this time. The point is that we record our thoughts. However, we only focus on what we must possess to approach the end of this iteration. This enables us to deliver on time and within budget.

One of the core operational procedures built into the agile approach is the daily stand-up. Members of the agile team stand up for a few minutes each morning to summarize progress. Problems and solutions are discussed, and they foresee and what they expect to achieve today.

The stand-up allows the team to provide input. It additionally allows for discussion about the progress being made to continue to deliver on the goal within the time and budget constraints as agreed. From this, the team manager can determine what resources or further compromises may be needed to get to the point of the creation of successful delivery.

A similar approach can be adopted for customer management. Perhaps daily, perhaps weekly.

In addition, when reviewing smaller projects, we can more accurately appraise the staged requirements. Determining what we are likely to achieve at a specific level and allowing time for each stage. This is known as time-boxing and provides another clue to the way progress is happening.

Utilizing smaller time increments is another way for the team to track short-term progress. All the following are reasonably straightforward but vital and can be time-boxed or planned out in terms of cost and time as phases: Pre-project, Feasibility, Foundations, Deployment (assemble/review/deploy), and post-project. The Post-project phase is supremely important as this is where the work is evaluated by management. It is possible to review outcomes and costs to ensure that we have kept to the time and budget constraints. To get a global view on the cost-effectiveness or value of investment. We want to know if the value is being delivered, and if adjustments are required.

Disrupt and march on

Ongoing feedback can be given back to the team. Changes in mission, and hopefully, a continuation of the project and agreement to the upcoming turn of iteration with a set of specific objectives.

This approach is far from reckless, and it can encourage an entrepreneurial spirit often missing from established businesses. Spirited start-ups can race out of the blocks as they may have enthusiasm and aptitude to make it work. Older, established companies are focused on execution, and their shape and nature are often resistant to change. They tend to focus on waterfall project management systems.

This is how to disrupt and revolutionize the way industry operates. Straightforward examples are shopping online. This industry has benefited massively since the outbreak of covid. National governments have ordered lockdowns and advised the public to reduce mingling with others and work from home.

It is expected over time, looking forward, there will be more of us working from home in the future, too.

The agile approach is straightforward to invest in and fund. If you are starting out it may cost little in terms of cash and may take appropriate time.

Very often, to start out, we need to develop a concept and set it together as an idea in our PowerPoint presentation, you then go promote the project. In doing so, you would demonstrate your ability in the field of service. Potentially, you would be the sole person who conceives the idea. Which, if the customer is interested, may position you in the ideal position as the exclusive supplier.

That leaves time and money. In most cases, you would agree on an affordable budget, depending on the needs and interests of customers. The timescale would normally be set by the customer, too. I typically set expectations by staging a project out over time and talk about first focusing on proof of concept and the need to assemble a private team.

Our customers can evaluate whether to manage this in-house or via my team. Generally, clients like the idea of the detail remaining my business and not something they desire to be troubled by. I tend not to talk to clients about saving money through overseas outsourcing, as this can become an expensive option if things go wrong.

Control is the key and, personally, I prefer to agree to things I can do or at least understand enough. Therefore, if necessary, I can roll up my sleeves and really get involved. Generally, I prefer to project manage rather than roll up my sleeves, although some customers find it reassuring to hear.

I have run projects like these on customer sites and even with customer staff. This is where you act as a consultant and steer a project and where you will have personal knowledge of an area of core competency. It can be lucrative, and it can continue for months and years. I prefer these opportunities to maintain two built-in options. The first of these is to limit the number of days per week. The second is, although I may remain the lead consultant. I reserve the right to appoint a colleague who, with the client's agreement, could supervise the project with me.

In this way, you can build an expanding business over time with the opportunity to grow through the development of a consulting team. However, you do need to vet your team and ensure they agree with your terms and conditions. Explicitly agree not to work with the client on any project directly. For good measure, you should additionally require the client to agree not to hire members of your team. Yet should they do so, they will be obliged to pay an exorbitant fee for the benefit as compensation. Most will agree with these terms.

The beauty of managing projects in the way I have described is they require zero investment other than the initial time required to secure the contract. You can put yourself in a position where there are no competitors, you develop something creative and tailored where there is no competition.

Either the potential customer goes ahead now, later, or never. These remain the three options. On the odd occasion, it is never or later. In most cases, in my experience, it is rapid. As the customer requires, it is likely to receive the budget too.

Broadly, when it comes to pricing, I start with a monthly fee of five thousand bucks. This tends to cover upfront costs, my time, and potentially the cost of hiring a consultant to complete the work. In most cases, I urge the customer to pay upfront on the basis this keeps my costs and therefore the fee as low as possible.

I have been refused. In which case, I seek a 50% deposit required for me to fund the project. If a customer still has a problem, I explain I cannot supply services to slow and there are no payers. With all the most honorable intentions in the world, I have worked with other customers where I have agreed they pay in arrears, and sometimes they do. The competent ones pay 30 days later. The undesirable ones 60 days later and the terrible ones 90 days later or longer.

This means that five thousand bucks can absolutely get to twenty thousand rapidly and it is too much. I have not agreed to be my customer's banker. I am not providing a banking service. I am providing a project service. Where banking is not part of the service required unless they are prepared to agree to pay ten thousand a month. In this manner, I demonstrate that five thousand per month is the prepaid discounted rate.

You may regard finance as an embarrassing or a sensitive subject. I have concluded contracts where the amounts per month are in millions. It is all just numbers at the end of the day. All I can say is you have to say the words. I know they are difficult conversations. However, it is much more difficult if you go into business and are twenty thousand bucks the wrong way, even for a private project.

Twenty thousand bucks are chump change for an established, profitable business, and these remain the only kind of clients I want to talk to. Otherwise, chances are you will expend the money. You will not get rewarded and will have to pay for services out of your own pocket. You may unexpectedly find yourself in an insolvency court. Once more, it is a lot more effortless to engage in this conversation once you know you are the only horse in town.

If your customer has developed the idea with you and you have tailored the presentation to accommodate only you, you leave the customer no alternative. You can dictate terms.

In any event, the entire project is for their benefit. As an exclusive result of your work, they should see themselves receiving a massive return on their investment. So why should you assume all the risks? Indeed, asking for 50% upfront constitutes a shared risk. With only a 50% upfront payment, you may not feel inclined to hire anyone else to support the project other than yourself. Consequently, at a minimum, it is only your own time you are risking and not the fee of someone else you will have to pay, come what may.

The cash flow portion of the financial conversation is one you must accommodate early. You can be prepared with a fixed rate-card; however, this may well position your service as a commodity. Or you can say you charge a consultancy-based day rate. The first day is free and is the total of your investment in them as the first day is typically devoted to defining the requirements.

You may prefer saying the first call or the first hour is free. It depends on you. Many solicitors tend to offer the first hour free. Certainly, no matter what you promote, the first portion of a discussion is routinely a discovery period. Discovery is where two parties, potential customers, and suppliers, get to know each other's interests and requirements.

Online, you may offer a free course, for instance, so there is no financial conversation. Although you are likely at the end of the course to want to introduce the delegate to a paid program. There you will explain what is on offer and how much the price will be.

If you are promoting products and not services, then there will be no price discussion, as your product will clearly be marked accordingly. However, if you are promoting a product, you are most likely not in a no-money-down business. As the product invariably needs to be paid for in advance. Unless you are fortunate as I was with my keyboard business. I found a manufacturer who was so successful, they merely extended me credit as a way of doing business. They were obviously desperate to convince a customer, any customer. Ultimately, it worked for all involved.

Therefore, as you may have gathered, selling services on a small team basis can represent a genuinely effective way of winning potentially large clients who can be extremely lucrative. I once set a target of ten thousand bucks per week. It looked like a lot at the time, and so I really pushed myself. One day, after securing a business, I realized I had more than surpassed the target. I was billed fifty thousand bucks a week.

By then, I was heading multiple small teams providing a range of outstanding services by hiring experts and I found the people I needed mostly on LinkedIn. I simply searched for people who appeared to possess the exact kind of experience required. I asked them if this type of work was something they would consider or if they had encountered anyone they could recommend. I elicited some favorable responses.

I did not hire everyone, and many did not reply at all. I would invite them to sign a non-disclosure agreement, brief them and then take them to be interviewed by the customer. I would usually put forward a single recommendation for each role.

This approach enabled me to build a Weboptimiser. Where the name of the firm was set to be as generic as possible. Initially, we merely wanted to do our bit to make the web a better place.

Over time, the business became synonymous with search engine marketing. A coincidence, which was for many years to our advantage. I have used another company name in parallel, which sounds like a Financial Services business. Yet, in fact, it is a consulting organization and works for financial-orientated clients.

You may still be wondering if what I have described comprises just a small team. Small teams keep costs and risks are low. A small team can be nimble. It enables fast customer decisions. A customer can scale up and down again. A fast decision may be necessary if there is a misinterpretation or movement of the goalposts (a problem, but only with certain clients). In addition, it means our price will be substantially lower than any price offered by a big consultancy. The convenience, personal attention, and flexibility we offer generally trumps outsourcing offshore.

In addition, a lower price of just a few thousand pounds per month can go ahead on a nod and not require a board decision. The board has likely already agreed to the overarching project, and a fee of a few thousand may be less than the cost of a line manager. For the money, the client gets an advisory service and a range of specific deliveries.

We may include a certain number of hours and then a rate per hour for additional hours. The idea is that the customer gets a monthly support service with consulting designed to take no longer than a few days per month.

Many types of work can be done. It can be C-level, accounting, payroll, recruitment, design work, assembly work, collation, research, fact-checking, development, test, security, and more. A service package can be based on any type of straightforward to the most sophisticated of services.

Remember, customers do not care about your size. How long you have been established or market size. They are interested in the same two things: time and money. It is their agenda we work on. Can you solve a problem for them? Can you improve their lives? On the odd occasion, for some clients, you do not have to do anything other than to support the operations by being an ear or an objective bouncing board.

If you have experience running a variety of diverse types of business, as I have. It has become possible to offer mentoring services where you are employed as a non-executive director. You are not a director, and you do not work in the business, you may work with an executive team on an external basis. You may support them to come to decisions, mediate, smooth the way, focus more on outcomes and objectives. It is possible you will help overcome problems or can review situations from an independent, impartial perspective.

All these service activities can mean you work from home, you do not have to hire anybody and instead you directly support the executives according to their needs.

You make the most money when you make the lives of your customers better. Be warned that if you make the lives of customers difficult, you will lose customers too. Customers tend to seize what you offer as gospel. They expect it, and even if it is modern and inspiring, it promptly becomes as expected. Potentially, boring as in been there, done that.

The key is to provide a service to improve customers' lives. Consequently, the emphasis must be on discovering ways where you can deliver proactive service, ways to surprise and purposefully delight and amaze customers.

Customers like to be interviewed or positioned at the center of things. I have discovered that U.S. entrepreneurs are good at this. One of the ways to deliver extra is to focus on enhancing and positioning value so it may be perceived more readily by your customers.

Frequently, we focus on improving the quality of a product and invest in the delivery of the product to make it better, to add value. This is tremendous unless your customer does not perceive it. Repeatedly, customers do not appreciate the value. They merely see order and delivery. They expect everything to be delivered and ideally do not desire to give it a second thought. Consequently, if you break your back to include extra quality in the product and your customers do not notice, what was the point?

You could detail the delivery elements in an invoice. That would be an excellent place to start, except you have limited space, plus your customers may not pay attention to the invoice. As all they must do is to sign it off and forward it for payment. Therefore, part of what we must build into our service delivery is communication. A classic way of achieving this is to deliver a client newsletter to keep customers and colleagues up to date on progress.

Personally, I like the idea of one month, a newsletter and the next month a special report, both containing insights. I also like delivering this kind of information by print, in the post, as it absolutely ensures delivery. Generally, to ensure 100% message delivery, use text messaging providing it is appropriate. The idea of switching content from month to month is to help stop customers from taking it for granted. The idea of print distribution is that few businesses provide anything in print. If you send a PDF, it might be glanced at. In the main, they are disregarded. So, print, and more especially, text messaging, has much more impact than email.

Predominantly, we want to win an initial foundation project. Such a project should deliver value to the customer and be profitable for us, too. It may be all we receive. There may be a change in heart. A project can stop in its tracks, and a customer may shift operations to a separate part of the world, this happens frequently.

For instance, I worked for years with Disney. One day, everything shifted to Paris. We got to the handover, and it was gone, all in a matter of weeks. Not just us and our project, the whole division shut down and shifted. New team, all new. Major restart. Anything can happen. All good things eventually come to an end. Similarly, all horses go lame at some point.

Next up: How to ask for new business. If you are still wondering about how you might find your first customer, the next chapter is provided to give you more insights into how it is done.

In chapter 9: How to ask for new business, you will discover:

- How to find your first, or next customer
- **Ask questions to convert customers to clients immediately**
- How to sell without being a salesperson
- **Why and how you should spend time focused on your client's favorite subject**
- How to develop and roll out your very first sales system

Chapter 9:

How to ask for new business

It is amazingly straightforward to acquire new customers, all you need to do is to ask for them.

Asking questions remains a number-one technique to get new business. Your first question can start innocuously with 'how do you do that? Followed up with a 'and how do you do that?' Most of us fail to ask, maybe we are apprehensive, or maybe we do not appreciate what to ask. Ask anything.

The key is not to start by telling others all about you. The key is to take an interest in them, to find out what they require, what they are interested in, to unearth what it is they might invest in. It is not about what you sell, it is about what the customer needs and wants and might buy.

Your questions will express your interest in them and should lead to the contribution of an idea or two about how you think their objectives may be achieved. This could lead to discussions on improving their situation. If the improvement is possible, and they react warmly to your suggestions, the chances are you will find a link to make a sale.

Broadly, most new services or products are defined to overcome a problem, usually enhancing efficiency, speed, or safety. This could be to do with leakage, material consumption or better patient care. The problem defines the solution, not the other way around.

We need to ascertain what the person cares about: whether they possess the capability to buy or are they someone of influence. To put it succinctly, we want to talk to the M.A.N. the person with the Money, Authority and Needs.

In effect, we want to ask our questions to establish the need, confirm authority and the final batch of questions may be concerned with pricing. A straightforward question is, how much would you be prepared to pay? The answer may positively surprise you.

What type of customization would you expect or require? How much would you expect to pay? Once more, you might be surprised with the answer. The answer may be higher or lower than your expectations. Higher sums are likely to be quoted relative to the level of desire.

160

Some may laugh at your questions, as they have played along. They may not genuinely require what you are working on. You can still ask them what they would take seriously, or what the problem they have or foresee. Every so often, people are just nervous and want to avoid being trapped.

Either way, you should leave the meeting, zoom, or phone call with an idea of the level of need and the price someone is willing to pay. An elementary mistake for start-ups is to offer a service or product for free on the basis they could become beta customers. This almost never works out.

Free offers do not validate genuine interest. You could well be lined up for excessive development, where the prospect discovers they can have anything and everything they want for free. This frequently ends up as a lose-lose proposition, with neither side getting what they want.

Alternatively, you succinctly state you are seeking a customer who has the means and interest to pay. Jointly, you can arrange a schedule where you will execute the plan and deliver a minimum specification system at the most inexpensive price. Probably lower than the amount they suggested. As might be expected, they can pay more for more features.

Naturally, the supplier should positively over deliver on the initial promise. Profit should not be your initial motive, although there is no harm in it. Your initial motive should be to ensure you have the most delighted customer, where costs at least are covered. Once you have a happy customer, you can create a case study. With this knowledge, you can adjust your pricing to make it worthwhile, with the confidence and evidence you can deliver again.

More preliminary questions should have informed you about customer requirements. If the objective is to enhance patient care, find economy or efficiency, you should have asked for the numbers. How many patients? How much will it save? How efficient does it need to be? How are things inefficient now? The answers will assist you with your cost justification and indeed the ability to quote Return On Investment (R.O.I.). Ask potential customers what other ratios they are interested in.

If a customer is genuinely interested in your offer, they will encourage you to build out your proposal. Potential customers should be inspired by what your delivery to their business will mean. In turn, it should demonstrably help them and their customers or patients.

No-trick Selling!

Beyond being an apprentice, I devoted two years trying to get into Xerox and eventually got in.

My main interest was due to their reputation for delivering amazing sales training, and I was not disappointed. Clyde Britton was my rock star trainer, and he was amazing. What I discovered, the amazing trick, was merely to be engaging, and normal. To build relationships.

There were no tricks. I was disappointed, at first. I had heard of the 'half-Nelson' and other ways to sell. I expected the foot in the door, where you hold the door ajar with your foot, to be a big part of it, but those techniques were simply not there. Clyde instructed us to be open, to pass comments about the time of day, the weather, anything, open to normal, everyday, natural conversation. Anti-sales with a firm focus on generating sales. I found it worked wonders as it is a different approach to what most might expect.

The sales area I was awarded was a renown and an exceptionally tough 'patch'. It was not a pleasant place, one of the largest industrial areas in the UK: Slough Industrial Estate.

I would drive in early in the morning, park and spend the day on foot. Door to door was hard graft. I would not tell them who I was or offer a business card and neither would I leave a brochure, mainly because I did not carry them. I looked like many other everyday executives. I had shiny shoes and I wore a suit, nothing more. I would typically arrive with a smile and ask what they did and let them know I thought it was fascinating.

162

David Whites' Start-up Rule #9
Be big on empathy and develop rapport.

Most of these businesses were so used to receive callers like me, they would place sentries on the door. Those sentries had an extremely boring job. I would go and talk to them and most of them would talk back, usually with words they did not require anything today. I would respond with a smile and universally agree with them. They would soon know I understood their objective and they were performing an excellent job.

I found the more charming and disarmingly I behaved, the more 'human', especially to the male sentries, the further I would get. They were delighted to devote a few minutes to me. The women were more capable of ignoring my charms. I guess they maintained a more spirited defense although I employed the same tactics and, in truth, most of those chats would go nowhere.

Some, most, had to enquire ultimately who I was representing and were quite surprised to discover I was from Xerox, a photocopier company. As most photocopier salespeople were much more aggressive. Some provided me with a chance and inquired why Xerox was better than say, Canon. That was a straightforward answer. Xerox focuses on the job at hand and has a simple operating panel you can get a lot done with. Xerox machines are simply more intuitive, therefore faster, joyful, and easier to use. Most people who had a Canon knew their machines had a control panel like a mission control flight deck. I would instantly discover if I had a Canon prospect on hand. This was tremendous information, as the primary challenge was always to extend Xerox contracts and change Canon machines out.

The next day, I would target a separate area of the same estate. Eventually, at some point in the month, a few weeks later, I would start at the beginning again. This time, some of the sentries would recommend me and say they hoped I would be back, they were waiting, as they had someone to introduce me too.

Some positively introduced me and, sure enough, some would say their 'sentry' had spoken favorably of me. There is extraordinarily little to trump genuine need. If you can be genuinely, super nice in a natural way, then pleasing others and being courteous can pay so much in dividends. It took me a long time to absorb this wholesome lesson. I would not say I am the most charming person in the world. Suffice to say, I model myself on James Bond, Miss Moneypenny. And laugh at my own jokes.

Add certainty with a questionnaire

In an earlier life, as I transitioned from the electronics industry, I won a design agency account handler contract. I looked after and found new clients. It was a complex role, there was a lot to lose, most of what we did was to be nice and take orders.

Some clients knew they had ongoing needs and had predetermined that all designs would be put through a sole preferred agency. This would typically be the case if the agency had done a great job of creating their branding and owned all the original artwork.

It made sense to clients and the agency relied on the repeat business. The designers were busy. They were not able to attend every single client meeting. A client manager was needed, and I was the only one for this medium-sized agency. There was increasingly a lot of back-and-forth meetings between the designer and the client.

It could get complex and so I became exceptionally skilled at taking notes and working with clients and designers. I developed a generic questionnaire to record answers to all the questions likely to arise.

The questionnaire meant taking a little longer with clients, yet all the information required was acquired. I routinely found extraneous details and depth to help tailor our work to customize the customer story.

Clients treasured the experience, and, over time, billing went up. It did not take long for the agency to put me on new business tasks. The stage was always set, the objective of the first client meeting was to run through the questionnaire.

Going in with a questionnaire was thorough, professional, and consultative. It developed to become 8-pages long. So long it could take a few hours to complete and new clients would be complementary to our thoroughness.

As a result of the amount of time spent addressing the client's favorite subject, themselves, we would develop a remarkably intimate bond. Our business winning strike rate for business development was extremely high. We did not consistently receive the billing we wanted from every client. Yet, we won the clients. The process eventually enabled us to work with the client to influence billing levels.

Raise your prices

To get the billing up to loftier levels, it was a straightforward matter of targeting more prominent firms and upping the ante. We found more ways to describe the questionnaire and employed terms like comprehensive review. We would ask if their existing agency ever offered them anything like this? We rightly assumed we knew the answer, no.

We stood out, not just because our design work was better, but because our approach was more insightful, innovative even. We built a perception from the very beginning. We focused on their details. In devoting much more time to new customers, up front, we were perceived as being better. The truth was, we had nothing better to do with our time.

Your very 1st sales system

You can get to a point where you mount a campaign to drive interview meetings to devote time to the initial client development sales process. It is such a valuable process it is worth incorporating into a streamlined asset.

This approach has worked across a wide range of businesses. It is obvious why. The more time you can devote to a prospective client, or cause a prospective client to engage with you, the better.

I have noticed that quite a few online businesses use similar techniques. However, the number of questions asked is less, and as it is not in person, their effectiveness will be lower.

The best position is always face-to-face; however, online questionnaires can still be powerful. They need to be fast and simple to complete and provide feedback or results quickly.

Online, you cannot focus on the mundane, which is an element of the face-to-face process when you are physically filling in a form with someone. Online serves the purpose of filtering prospects in or out of a given lane of interest, as a pre-qualifier. This leads to an in-person meeting, which nowadays can also be delivered via skype or similar.

You may have noticed that asking questions is not a sales pitch. The point is not to talk about what you promote, it is also not to demonstrate how much knowledge you have. This is extremely critical to avoid if you are not an expert.

We cannot pretend to be experts at something we are not experts at. Yet we can gather information and ask for and express our opinions, and we can discuss best practice, for instance. Principally, we want to know when and how much it is costing the client to not address the key issues they deem the need for.

You may be aware that most buying is done emotionally. We purchase a car based on what it looks like and how we would feel to be seen driving it. If we can enhance the feeling for technical reasons, all the better. But, if the look of the thing does not satisfy our expectations of how we would like to be seen, we will not consider the possibility and certainly not consider further technical information.

When we ask questions, we invite conversation. As a salesperson we can be much more effective when we listen with our two ears and speak in proportion, with one mouth. If a client likes blue, we can talk about why blue works. We can also introduce light, dark, and electric blue. We might be capable of justifying and focusing on blue more. Or we could investigate why we would want to be the same color as a rival or potentially be confused with the blue of an emergency service if that is appropriate.

We can ensure that our mutual viewpoint or understanding of needs is sharpened and aligned. Our understanding of key issues or problems can be tuned to transport us to a place where we are more likely to identify solutions. Chances are we will learn more about each other and feel served, moved (ideally) emotionally, supported and potentially fulfilled.

We should aim to leave our discussions energized and look forward to the future together with the certain knowledge we are doing the right thing. Getting answers to many pertinent questions can ensure the client feels that a good briefing has been delivered. In addition, the client is unlikely to want to invest a similar amount of time with a competitor. The chances of a competitor taking notes in a similarly orderly and professional manner are unlikely.

Many ways to ask for new business

The first way to ask for new business is indeed to ask. Ordinarily, the best way to ask is to first be nice about something relevant. Perhaps something the potential customer has said or published. All you need to do is to mention what you have learned and why it is critical. The chances are you will stand out like few others.

The key is to work out why it is urgent to ask this person, beyond the fact you want to sell something. We all want to sell something; your communication will become more meaningful if you can state why you are interested and why this individual might be ideal to work with. Write down why you want to talk to the potential client. What have they stated or done you might find interesting to ask about and seek a connection? How can this assist you both in the future?

Similarly, work out what they require to achieve, what their goals may be. See if you can obtain a statement or a presentation or a press release that expresses their wishes for the future. For each occasion, for each person, work out how you can support them with their goals.

This additionally becomes something you should mention when you manage to communicate with them and can serve to construct the basis of a deeper bond between you. It may be impossible to approach the person on the phone. Yet it may be possible to convey ideas, suggestions, articles, books, or anything else you may match to their objectives through other mediums and means.

It does not have to be all serious, there are other ways to connect with people, through humor, through family, through connections, even. Every so often, a lot of time can pass between meetings. All sorts of things can get in the way, holidays, emergencies, other business, interviews, training programs, product launches and so on.

Most of us carry around two agendas, our work agenda and a home or personal agenda. It is sometimes challenging to distinguish between the two, yet the two agendas' sit side by side. You may find out about one, be aware there is another.

Certain knowledge of the existence of another agenda may trigger a deeper relationship, and friendships become personal.

Understanding the agenda is key to forming lifelong friendships and an enduring effective relationship. There are some direct questions you can ask: What are your objectives for the end of this year? What are the significant goals you look to bring home? What will the activities involve you in the next few months? What are you most excited about completing or achieving?

Get out of your comfort zone

You may have heard you are the sum of the people you surround yourself with. I would suggest you accomplish more than surrounding yourself with good people. It is a clever idea to surround yourself with those who are different from you to get out of your natural comfort zone. In this way, you will no doubt discover or explore strange and unprecedented opportunities. Just one of those could produce a considerable difference to your success. It could be certain people set you on edge, yet they may be the kind of people who could steer you in some remarkably unusual directions.

I live in London and have some remarkably unusual associates who are solidly from Essex, I am not from Essex, and we speak and think differently. When I initially encountered them, they screeched like chalk on a blackboard, and I found it difficult to tune in. Everything just seemed mad, preposterous, mountains made from molehills, what was important to them was unimportant to me. The world was upside down. They absolutely maintained a completely conflicting perspective on life and yet we lived in the same city.

I persisted with what seemed like jaw dropping madness of drinks, mayhem, football, and partying in and around Chelsea. Not a million miles from where I live. I was, at first and predominantly, an observer. I am not from Essex and behave, by and large, differently. Their views are different. They transported me into a parallel, prosperous and influential world, so different from my normal.

Who do you appreciate who is altogether different? Who would challenge you? In just the same way, I have strong Muslim, Jewish, and Christian acquaintances. Groups of people who I love to pieces. Yet, I will likely never become a devout believer in the same way myself. These differences unite us, the knowledge we are not the same. There is an instinct to maintain our relationships. This has led to being invited to an enormous range of events, not only in the capital where I live. Also, across the U.K., Europe, and many in the U.S., even to my first baseball game.

The key to sound new business is to develop stable relationships. Substantial relationships are developed merely by submitting intelligent questions. It can be possible to do some business quickly if other people retain respect for you. So, the stronger and deeper your relationship, the better. It can be harsh to be all in with someone you do not appreciate, expectations may be different, first impressions may not be genuine and can alter. In most cases, a marriage progresses nicely. Yet some should work, yet do not last. Typically, this is because the foundations of a relationship are assumed and not deep enough.

Hanging around long enough to ask questions and to get answers and to get to test them can lead to a solid relationship. Therefore, it is important to take your time. It is understandable in the short term to want to move fast.

Next up is How to write an ad for your business: we will run through how to write an advertisement, which will help you organize your presentations to increase your chances of closing the deal.

In chapter 10: How to write an advertisement for your business, you will discover:

- How to see through the 'eyes' of a potential customer
- **How to and why you should get to know who you are targeting**
- How you will save time by following the classic ad structure
- **How to employ your advertising strategy in all you do**
- Which works best – long or short copy?
- **The best style for your ads and what else you can harness to give your ad extra power**

Chapter 10:

How to write an ad for your business

Attract attention, generate interest

Before you do anything else, write an ad.

The objective of an ad is to sell potential customers on the idea they should act. You are looking for a financial act. Sales only occur when someone makes a purchase. Free trials, likes, shares and five-star reviews are great, but they fail to cut it.

Social media and search provide a broad platform for acquiring customers but be certain you focus on sales. Likes and shares are good to demonstrate social currency, but you cannot bank them or buy a house.

Many people squander time, focusing on the incorrect results. Achieving seemingly for achievements sake. Be aware of spending time performing activities where the results do not include the generation of new money. It is easy to be a busy fool. It seems possible to target those who like to purchase digital products. If this is the appropriate audience for you, then you need to persuade them to buy from you too. Decades of experience tells me most play with technology and achieve little.

A high-end, famous French fashion marketing heavyweight made it very clear to me, and her brand did not want to be easy to find. Easiness was not the essence of her brand. She was very certain if her brand was more easily found, her prices would tumble. Being exclusive was her brand's key characteristic. In her case, I must agree, I think she was right.

In utilizing digital marketing technology, most customers have little to sell. Those who do tend to last. Everyone else employs digital marketing for reasons of PR or pride, far less sales.

If you have a brilliant idea for a product or service, you must think about who will acquire it if you want to be successful as well. Writing an ad is an efficient way to work out exactly how you will convert interest into sales. You will also discover how to develop and diversify a product range or service. Through writing an ad, we look at our ideas through the eyes of a potential customer. Invariably, we will discover a treasure trove of information.

A sale goes beyond what is being sold to who you are selling to and why. It is worth writing out who and why. Know the customer cannot be everyone, you must focus on someone. If you do not focus on a specific person, you will not be effective at stating what you have for them clearly.

It may be a person with a certain problem, or interest. This may dictate age, gender, role, and so on. You may determine they are likely to have or want children, or their children are long gone, or children are irrelevant. By narrowing your field of view to a particular type of audience, you will be more capable of positioning yourself as being for them. This is vital to maximize sales and minimize costs.

We will never attract everyone's interest as it is prohibitively expensive to advertise to all, think TV budgets. If we appreciate exactly who we prefer to target, we may be able to reach them directly, and usually, inexpensively too. Through online media, for instance, LinkedIn, where perhaps we could find qualified prospects one by one.

Instead of the shotgun approach to target everyone, you are more likely to achieve success with a rifle where you can aim for a particular person. You want your target to believe you are for them as soon as they see you.

Later, when we have achieved initial sales, we might expand the approach. From profits generated, you could purchase advertising or lists and target them more systematically, on a larger scale. First, step 1, you need to be laser clear on who you are targeting. Start by writing out and getting as clear as you can, with as much detail as you know about who you want to target.

We want to pinpoint and minimize the target opportunities to test our hypothesis and to increase our chances of success.

Potential customers are interested in knowing more about who they are buying from, too. In this case, this is you. You must allow potential customers to appreciate why what you promote is worthwhile and why you are the best at offering it. Step 2 is to write out, or bullet point, why you are right for them.

You will force yourself to think about client needs if you commit yourself to writing an Ad. Writing an ad can be quite sobering. You may uncover a fundamental flaw in your approach. As a result, you may need to implement changes. Better now than never.

Now is a great time to make those necessary changes before you get too far ahead. Before you expend more time and potentially cash to support your new business idea. You want to be as sure as you can be for your efforts to be rewarded. It is better to undertake a project with a probable outcome, than to pursue one on the basis that it might.

If you discover a fundamental flaw, stop, but do not worry. You have found an objective you need to overcome. Often a brilliant idea if you are incapable of swiftly resolving the issue is to sleep on the problem. Allow your mind to consider diverse ways, around, over or under.

The issue may steer you back to the drawing board, which may delay your plans. Better than to continue headlong into a disaster, there is a bright side! As one door shuts, two more always open, you just have to find where they are.

Ad Structure

Fortunately, ads possess a structure, and ad structure is reasonably straightforward. The ad structure starts with a headline, is followed by a subhead, potentially a list of bullet points, a picture, and a call to action. Usually, but not always in that order. Sometimes, a picture comes first.

If you find an ad, one you admire, you can model it. Ideally, it will not come from the same target market. Typically, the resulting ad represents the condensed version of everything you want to say to your prospects. You must also try to make your ad interesting, entertaining, direct perhaps and punchy.

176

You should employ your ad copy in more ways than one. If you supply packaged goods, make sure your copy flows onto the packaging. Collectively, the general image conveyed should flow through to your product design. You want to ooze consistency to reflect brand quality. Provide your customers with what they expect, and you will build on your brand trust too.

If you do not produce packaged goods, there are still ample opportunities to use the copy in a range of places, from social media stories to apparel.

Most copy fitting is unnatural, forced by size constraints. The truth is, and many tests have proven this long copy sells. A long copy possesses all the attributes of a short-form ad plus a story. In a story, the key issues are most likely to be spelled out. In long copy you may have the opportunity to employ more pictures and add detail to embellish an important point. There are likely case studies or use cases you can employ and potentially testimonials from previous customers too.

How an ad looks

While we are talking about writing an advertisement, it does not have to look like an ad.

Essentially, anything a potential customer reads or hears about you should lead to an outcome. Where the outcome is to generate sufficient interest to obtain and close customers.

This should be the case, even in conversation. How an ad looks need to be tested. Famously David O'gilvy favoured a headline, a large picture, followed by copy. When you have to pay for space, many decide to drop the picture.

Often, you discover longer copy ads sell more. Also, counter intuitively ugly ads can convert more too. However, many enterprises have brand guidelines and a decided image to adhere to which are designed to provide comfort for regular customers to believe your enterprise is well run, efficient, smart and organised. Each organisation will have it's own values. The company has to decide what it wants more. Sales or comfort? There will be a trade off.

Writing style

Your writing style should be informal, perhaps casual, certainly familiar, helpful, as if talking to a friend or someone you know. As far as possible, your advertisement should match your personality, especially if they must contact you to make a purchase, you want to avoid culture shock. Hence, for instance, if you can be humorous, use humor.

Stilted, official text has its place, and the place is rarely in an advertisement. Customers do not like to be told to buy. Yet, your copy needs to be assertive. It is critical for you to explain what the subsequent steps are and urge the person you are talking to, to take them.

The content of your ad

Chances are there is a lot of information you will not have, like case studies and testimonials. However, you can always employ use cases. A use case represents a description of how to utilize your service from a customer's perspective.

Right now, you may be aghast at the idea of writing. You may be reaching for your contacts to investigate if you are associated with a copywriter. Yet a copywriter would start by needing to know the answers to the following questions:

Who are you targeting?

Why would they be interested?

A copywriter will need to know more about why the product or service you provide is so good or so much better than what could be available elsewhere.

There is nothing wrong with hiring a copywriter, however, if you are starting out, you may not want to afford one. There are various ways to start. One of the best ways to start is to imagine you are having a conversation with a friend and start by resolving those questions.

Use your phone for speed

If you do not want to write, you do not have to. If you cannot think of a headline, do not worry either. Here is a suggestion:

Take your phone, turn the camera on and run through the key questions below. Talk as if you were having a conversation with a friend. Use natural language and focus on answers, not grammar.

No one else will review the video unless you share.

None of us like the sound of our own voices. By the way, you do not have to overhear it by playing it again. Merely talk, talk about the subject, answer the questions, describe in detail what your product or service is and what the benefits are. Use the following checklist for topic and content ideas:

Conversational checklist

1. Who would want it?
2. Why would they want it?
3. What does it do?
4. How does it do that?
5. Why would it do that in that way?
6. What is so important about it?
7. Describe how and why yours is better?
8. How will it save time?
9. How will it save money?
10. Why does it do a better job?
11. How configurable is it?
12. Who are all the people who would use it?
13. What headline ideas can I quickly think of?
14. What are the key features of this service or product?
15. What are the key benefits this service or product offers?

Extract the text

Open a YouTube account and load up your video privately. Once it is uploaded, select subtitles and everything you say in the video will be generated as a text file in a few minutes. You may want to prepare a coffee or brew a cup of tea while you wait.

Take a break, you have earned it and clear your head for a few minutes. When you come back, the file should be ready and there will be some editing to do.

You will find a block of text. Cut it and paste it into a word processor of your choice and quickly go through it. Take out the 'ums', the 'ars', and maybe delete the odd wayward sentence, sentiment, or now inappropriate statement. Clean it up.

Some of what you said may not make sense when you see it in writing. In this case, you may have to go back and listen to a portion of what you said, heaven forbid.

Before long though, you will have translated what was said into a coherent and readable form.

You may be surprised at how easily possible this was, how little time it took, and how many words there are.

Now, you have the basis of what you need. Go through the checklist again and see what you can add and edit the list. Expand it out to make the biggest, longest document you can.

Maybe discuss the text with a colleague or customer for greater insights and an alternative point of view. If you decide you can afford it, take what you have worked out and use it as the basis for a brief to give to a copywriter. A good brief will help you get the results you want. A copywriter cannot have too much information. Usually, a copywriter does not have enough information.

This is what we call long copy, if it is logical and flows in an informal style, it may even be serviceable, probably not yet without some additional editing. I would think about it for a day or two, covering all the angles could be critical.

It is in this process you hone, tune and further cement who you are for, which is the key to getting the sales you want.

Only when you have every angle covered and more, can you think about crafting an initial headline. You may come up with several. You may want to grab a newspaper or magazine (or both) and look at the headlines the professional's use. You may want to order them according to what you think customers may be most interested in.

If you have partners or potential customers, ask them to assist you in prioritizing your list, this is critical. We want to test the headlines, understand how others might react. One thing is that our headlines do not want to be too tricky or difficult. Readers need to understand what is going on immediately. Do not try to be too clever, do not feed them with a puzzle, as they will not bother to work it out, your copy should be easy to understand, otherwise all your efforts will most likely be wasted.

We must put the winning headlines in order, with the most interesting, most worthwhile to the client, biggest benefit items first. Once you have prioritized, you may be talented enough to pick through to edit the first paragraph.

The objective of the headline is to attract interest and develop intrigue. A simple technique is to use the headline to pose a question in the mind of the recipient. Ideally a tease. This is one way for your readers to feel compelled to want to read on and find out more. The headline and each paragraph should deliver more value, inform the reader something truthful and, at each stage, tease the reader to read on.

David Whites' Start-up Rule #10
Start conversations with intrigue

You should end up with a headline and multiple paragraphs. See if you can order or group the paragraphs as this will help you come up with sub heads. When you have finished adding subheads, read over them. See if the subheads make sense, see if they flow. Could a reader get the gist of your copy from the headline and subheads alone? It is a brilliant idea to make it so they can, as it increases the readability of your copy.

Above all, your copy should not be difficult. If you use Word and there is a review function, you want to aim for a low readership score. Ideally, even a child should be capable of understanding your copy. We do not want to impress readers with long words, technical terms, or jargon, as doing so will exclude many readers and reduce the effectiveness of your efforts.

Think about your 'why'

You may want to think more about your reasons. As mentioned earlier, customers pay attention to not only what your product or service is, but also who they might be buying it from. For many, this is the most important part. You may find the book 'Start With Why' by Simon Sinek useful for inspiration, or his YouTube videos.

Your 'why' will be most important to the people you pitch to.

By the time you have finished, the objective is to have a rounded out and thought through proposition. Know who you are and why you are sufficiently different for them to invest in you. What is to stop them from getting things done in-house? Of course, all customers retain those options. It is up to you to explain why they are the poorer choice and yours is the superior offer.

This exercise should reveal whether your initial ideas are perfect, or it may have highlighted some areas to improve upon or embellish. You should have clues about how to further develop this business and how to create diverse streams of income too. This is important, as multiple income streams give you more opportunities to stabilize and grow your business.

Being able to tell others about your ambition may help others understand and believe your passion and commitment to the business. Your passion and commitment are essential to building trust in all new business start-ups.

You have all you need to brief a writer or designer should you need.

You may also have the basis for a book or a guide.

My suggestion is to take the headings and consider the notes you have written under each and write three paragraphs as an exercise; you may be surprised at just how much this adds if you have never done this before.

You can write or talk it on your phone again and run the YouTube trick to extract the text. The paragraphs you want are an opening, a middle piece, the meat, and a closing paragraph. You may change the order or add additional headings and paragraphs to suit.

I would suggest, however, you open with the biggest benefits to the client first. Tie your why to the biggest benefit. The idea is to end up with a multi-page booklet. You should be able to expand each item by including use cases and case studies if you have them. Case studies can work with or without client names, plus potentially, testimonials too. However, these are more believable the more detail you can offer. Name, date and place them as often as you can, when it comes to testimonials, the more you tell, the more you sell.

Note, usually the more you tell in person, the less you sell. In writing, information can be skipped, although in writing all the detail is there and some may well buy based on the bulk and read the headings and sub-heads alone. Some are impressed by the thud factor.

Before you know it, you will have quite a body of work. This is an asset. The type of asset you will most likely refer to again and again.

Now, you have become an expert who knows all about the subject. You should write a book to demonstrate your expertise.

When it comes to pitching and selling, collateral landing with a thud is powerful. A well thought through document will clearly demonstrate your credentials. This is important to demonstrate your leadership potential. Good, sensible content can make the barrier to entry higher for competitors. Chances are, they will not have anything like this to hand and certainly not have thought through their business the way you have.

Sometimes I have seen people write out just a page, it's a great start. My thoughts on this are you can always add more later. The more you write, the better it will tend to work for you. A book would be one hundred and twenty pages long, for instance. It could be forty, it could be three hundred. Many people like books and, surprisingly, many do not get around to reading all the books they buy...

Written proof

The key is to start by writing an ad.

Writing an ad will help you to build out your case and demonstrate commitment, as well as show others what you think about your business ideas. Seeing a business plan in writing is often all the proof an investor (or client) needs to see.

The power of words on paper is incredible. Even though it is simply your idea in writing. However, this seemingly small step means much to many. It would seem, as a human race, we find words in print very persuasive. Perhaps it is because we are used to see contracts, agreements, instructions, and orders in writing.

Your investors may well be your customers. When you write an ad, it will motivate you, and others who read it, including potential customers and investors. You will have put your ideas down on paper, it will put words into your mouth too. You will have something to be proud of. Your confidence will be stronger. Your idea will literally expand in front of your eyes.

It is said a good business plan will write itself.

Thinking and writing about your product or service from your client's perspective is a key achievement.

184

This important step must precede the actual development of a product or service.

An ad can be very influential when it comes to product development. An ad can rapidly lead you toward more productive areas of opportunity without the need to spend a fortune on blind research and development (R & D).

Hiring a copywriter

Copywriters are professionals who write ads. Whether you write the ad or provide answers to the questions a copywriter asks about your product matters not. The clearer and more precisely you can provide those answers, the better and more usable will be the final copy. Chances are you will get more than one version to review.

Copywriters sometimes write treatments that show how one angle might work compared to another. This could be valuable. If you want to review copy written from several angles, you should advise the copywriter about this, or hire more than one copywriter. You may be surprised where this leads to, and you may discover angles you did not think were there. This can lead to entirely new business opportunities for you.

Customers: actual proof

In the short term, you can share your written efforts with your family, friends, and colleagues.

Chances are some will never read it. Some may critique it, some may add ideas to it for you, others will congratulate you, and someone might want to invest in it.

It is amazing what happens when you put your ideas down on paper.

Not only do you have the basis of a book. You may also have the basis of a business plan. With your idea in words, it will help you to visualize and provide further motivation to take your new business forward.

Perhaps you will change or adapt for additional use cases where you add even more functionality and diversify. The more the better. Perhaps you will create a family or range of products or services to fulfil certain customer needs.

To me, delivering a service or product to customers is the most important stage. Having a business plan and actual customers provides the ultimate proof of concept. With a proof of concept, you demonstrate you are on the right path and really do mean business.

The number of customers matters less than the fact you have some.

When you have customers, even if it is just one, you have proven a) you can sell and b) you have a genuine commercial opportunity.

If you have an ad outline in writing, you have all you need to prepare a PowerPoint slide deck. This will help you demonstrate your plan to potential customers, who would invest in you. They would look at you, look at what you had in mind, potentially agree with you, and want some or not.

If not, stay around long enough to find out why. What else do they want to see? What condition would you need to fulfil for them to become a customer? Questions... Questions...

To do business with you, a potential customer would have to place an order with you. You could ask for all, or a percentage upfront to cover the costs of further development to suit them.

You may be surprised (potentially shocked) to discover that some will agree and give you all the money you need.

Many of us like to be a part of something new and encourage entrepreneurs, especially if our client is part of a big successful organization.

Either way, cash is King. I, for one, have always been happy to offer a discount to anyone who pays upfront. As it avoids all the difficulties (and concerns and expense) of getting paid later. In any case, whenever possible, I have always outsourced debt collection to my bank.

More customers

When you have written your ad, especially a long-form ad, you have all you need to write a promotional copy for an editorial review or as a news release.

Again, you can hire a copywriter to write these for you too.

You can promote your product ahead of time and pre-sell it if the opportunity exists. Let people know what is coming. You could take deposits and store cash in a separate bank account if you wanted. Again, banks will lend against cash in the bank, money you generate they can now charge a fee for!

The opposite may be true

Also, and here's a sobering thought, you may write your ad, share it, and potentially discover the market is underwhelmed and few show interest.

Obviously, this is not the outcome you seek.

You may need to go back to the proverbial drawing board and redesign your product or your ad, or both.

Though negative, this is extremely valuable information to know. Information I would like to know sooner rather than later before I spend more time and effort. When we are at the advertisement writing stage, there is much, we can change, including choosing not to continue. This can save time and heartache early on before you become overly committed to a positive outcome expectation or worse: sunk costs.

It may turn out that you are the only person with any excitement about your proposition. It may be the things you are interested in are not the same as the market is interested in. This could lead you to change the product or service to something the market really wants.

It is not necessarily all bad news, invariably there is always some good news. If the outcome frees your time, you are free to move on to something more worthwhile.

Normally, the act of writing an ad strengthens and confirms thoughts.

You should strive to nail the benefits. You must discover at least three and, if there are more, find the three most valuable benefits to customers.

Sometimes, through the simple act of writing out an ad, you can discover that one key benefit overrides the others and discover yet more as a result. This is where you truly experience the power of writing an ad.

Afterward, you generally end up with so much more than you started with. This can only add to your passion and help to prove your conviction.

Chapter 11:

42 Growth Hacks

These hacks were devised by reviewing each of the chapters of this book.

For each hack, a 5 point bullet point summary is included extracted from 'Sales Strategies for Start-ups'. Due to feedback since the initial inclusion in this book, each hack has been updated and revised substantially as complete stand alone strategies you could use as a blueprint.

Also please visit the companion website https:// TheAuthorityFigure.com/ where you will find more on the topics in this book. You will also see a link to YouTube and Twitter accounts, too.

Hack #1: How smart business start-ups get customers to buy more on demand so cash flow worries are solved forever.

1: CONSIDER CUSTOMER INTERESTS

2: PREPARE SCRIPTS AND CHOREOGRAPHY

3: CONVERSATIONS START WITH SMALL-TALK

4: CONVERSATIONS GET BOGGED DOWN WITH HIDDEN AGENDAS

5: DEFAULT DIAGNOSIS, YOUR CUSTOMERS IDEAL SOLUTION

REFERENCE CHAPTER 2: TIME & MONEY

Hack #2: How the under appreciated can get to the top of their field and quickly command the attention of the market quickly

1: RESEARCH POPULAR BOOKS IN YOUR CHOSEN FIELD

2: RAPIDLY UPDATE YOUR KNOWLEDGE

3: BECOME A BETTER COMMUNICATOR

4: BECOME A RECOGNISED AUTHOR

5: CREATE SELF-LIQUIDATING OFFERS

190

Hack #3: How a beginner can learn a new subject and test new business opportunities

1: Review the market for training in your sector

2: Attract more beginners by offering training

3: Use training as a self-liquidating offer

4: Learn more about student needs

5: Promote your student project

Reference chapter 2: Time & Money

Hack #4: managers can educate the market to buy more from you without being a great writer

1: You can either write or use transcripts for content

2: You can deploy your resulting work in many ways

3: Books can be an unexpected blessing

4: Redeploy your work in many ways

5: You probably have all you need

Reference chapter 2: Time & Money

Hack #5: How business start-ups can drive the best quality inquiries who will pay more, stay longer, and be happier customers, more likely to refer

1: Talk about what you can do for your customers

2: Create how-to guides that resonate

3: Consider real client conversations

4: Convert conversations to assets

5: Build trust by using media

Hack #6: How do successful business owners focus on what customers want to buy so that their business expands and customer satisfaction is at an all time high?

1: FIND OUT WHAT YOUR AUDIENCE WANTS

2: THE BEST IDEA IS TO CUSTOMIZE SOLUTIONS

3: WANT MONEY? ASK CUSTOMERS TO PAY

4: FOCUS ON AUDIENCE NEEDS, BE DIFFERENT

5: REMAIN OPEN AND FLEXIBLE

REFERENCE CHAPTER 3: THE IMPORTANCE OF NO MONEY DOWN

Hack #7: As a business owner have you defined the essential stress tests to avoid starting a new venture that is bound to fail and waste time, money, and risk bankruptcy?

1: DOES MARKET DEMAND EXIST?

2: WILL POTENTIAL CLIENTS PAY FOR A SOLUTION?

3: WILL POTENTIAL CLIENTS PAY FOR MORE AND MORE?

4: CAN YOU GET AND STAY CLOSE TO ENOUGH CUSTOMERS?

5: ARE YOU INTO THE BUSINESS?

REFERENCE CHAPTER 3: THE IMPORTANCE OF NO MONEY DOWN

Hack #8: As a business manager are you aware you can boost sales by reducing waste, costs, and time delays to increase profits and customer satisfaction too?

1: DO YOU ASK CLIENTS FOR FEEDBACK

2: DO YOU TEST MINIMUM VIABLE PRODUCTS?

3: HAVE YOU EVER CONSIDERED APPLYING LEAN PROCESSES?

4: HOW MANY OF THE STEPS ARE ALREADY IN PLACE?

5: DO SALES DELIVER LOCKED-IN, HAPPY CLIENTS?

REFERENCE CHAPTER 3: THE IMPORTANCE OF NO MONEY DOWN

Hack #9: Are you a business owner who knows the five personal characteristics you must apply to ensure no money down success, eliminate high risk and guarantee high returns?

1: YOU PUT ENERGY INTO YOUR PLANS

2: YOU ACT AND FOLLOW THROUGH

3: YOU POSSES PASSION AND INTEREST

4: YOUR PRODUCT OR SERVICE SELLS

5: YOU ACT ON A MARKET STRATEGY

REFERENCE CHAPTER 3: THE IMPORTANCE OF NO MONEY DOWN

Hack #10: How smart business managers coordinate their marketing activity to deliver higher than normal return on investment so they can out-market their rivals

1: PLAN IN-DEPTH, NOT JUST THE ACTIVITY BUT THE MESSAGING

2: YOUR STRATEGY MUST BE AT THE HEART OF YOUR PLAN

3: HUB AND SPOKE MARKETING BUILDS TRUST

4: BE AN AUDIENCE-LED BUSINESS

5: ALLOW FOR MEASUREMENT

REFERENCE CHAPTER 3: THE IMPORTANCE OF NO MONEY DOWN

Hack #11: How do business owners get paid more for all their hard work so they can build the capital they need to cover for rainy days?

1: GET KNOWN FOR A SKILL YOU OWN

2: TWO ROUTES: ACTIVE OR PASSIVE

3: MAKE AND MAINTAIN CONTACT

4: BE THE SAVIOR

5: BE CONSISTENT

REFERENCE CHAPTER 4: SMALL STEPS CAN LEAD TO BIG LEAPS

Hack #12: How business managers create valuable assets to generate cash flow, get new leads, and self-finance promotions

1: How-to books are the biggest category

2: Create a series as an income stream

3: Produce assets for consumer use

4: Informational how-to are the key

5: Create and sell assets you own

Reference chapter 4: Small steps can lead to big leaps

Hack #13: Do you know where thought leaders go to get the insights they need to succeed while remaining current, thought-provoking, and on-topic?

1: Start with the obvious

2: Look through the lens of your audience

3: Interview those who have problems to resolve

4: There's no need to spend a fortune on recording

5: Talk to different sources, to build more resources

Reference chapter 4: Small steps can lead to big leaps

Hack #14: 5 ways to start a business with no money down, minimize risk and maximize the upside

1: LOOK FOR OPPORTUNITIES SUITABLE FOR MODERNIZATION

2: MAKE MORE DISCOVERIES THAN YOUR COMPETITORS

3: PROVIDE CONSULTING, ADVICE, AND TRAINING

4: SECURE YOUR COMMERCIAL FOUNDATION

5: SHARE YOUR INSIGHTS

REFERENCE CHAPTER 4: SMALL STEPS CAN LEAD TO BIG LEAPS

Hack #15: How can any business manager achieve more by speaking instead of writing, clearly, unambiguously and quickly to minimize cost and time overhead?

1: SPEAK INSTEAD OF WRITE (JUST HIT RECORD FIRST)

2: CONVERSATIONAL COMMUNICATION WORKS BEST

3: THERE ARE A SURPRISING NUMBER OF SPIN-OFFS

4: ON-BOARDING CUSTOMERS SETS EXPECTATIONS

5: TELL STORIES, AND GET CLOSER TO CLIENTS

REFERENCE CHAPTER 4: SMALL STEPS CAN LEAD TO BIG LEAPS

Hack #16: 5 ways for any business to attract premium clients who pay premium rates to avoid the swirl to the bottom that leads to failure and bankruptcy

5: THE HIGHER YOUR FEE, THE MORE CUSTOMERS CELEBRATE

4: SELLING LESS TO MAKE MORE IS A RECIPE FOR SUCCESS!

3: PREMIUM RATES APPLY TO PREMIUM CUSTOMERS

2: START BY PRODUCING PERSONALIZED PACKAGES

1: ATTRACTING PREMIUM PRICES IS A CHOICE

REFERENCE CHAPTER 5: THINK BIG, START SMALL, SCALE FAST

Hack #17: How to get more customers to come to you.

1: BEFORE ANYTHING ELSE, DECIDE WHO YOU ARE FOR

2: CULTIVATE CUSTOMER FLOW FOR THE MOST VALUED

3: OFFER EXCLUSIVE ACCESS BY INVITATION ONLY

4: CREATE CUSTOM SOLUTIONS AND PACKAGES

5: WORK WITH THE CREME DE LA CREME

REFERENCE CHAPTER 5: THINK BIG, START SMALL, SCALE FAST

Hack #18: How any business manager can expand their capability without increasing spending, going on a course, or hiring more staff?

1: LEARN FROM FAILURE, DON'T REPEAT THE MISTAKES OF OTHERS

2: YOU WOULD BE AN EDUCATED RESEARCHER ABLE TO ZONE IN

3: MOST ORGANIZATIONS CONTAIN UNTAPPED RESOURCES

4: THERE ARE PLENTY OF PLACES TO LOOK TO FOR HELP

5: WHO DO YOU KNOW, WHO COULD HELP YOU?

REFERENCE CHAPTER 5: THINK BIG, START SMALL, SCALE FAST

Hack #19: 5 ways to keep your customers delighted and discover new business opportunities without the risk of losing those existing clients

1: TALK TO YOUR CUSTOMERS BEFORE, DURING AND AFTER SALES

2: WE LIKE TO BE THANKED, RECOGNISED AND REWARDED

3: FOCUS ON TURNING REGULAR CUSTOMERS INTO CLIENTS

4: MEASUREMENT ALLOWS FOR DISCOVERABILITY

5: MEASURE CUSTOMER SATISFACTION

REFERENCE CHAPTER 5: THINK BIG, START SMALL, SCALE FAST

Hack #20: How business managers employ feedback systems to ensure business growth is well oiled and does not jam up due to small problems becoming big issues

1: COMMUNICATION IS THE PERPETUAL MOTION MACHINE OF GROWTH

2: THERE IS NO ONE-WAY TO INTERACT WITH CUSTOMERS

3: PERSONALIZE YOUR INTERACTIONS WITH CUSTOMERS

4: TAKE THE RIGHT ACTIONS BY YOUR CUSTOMERS

5: USE MANY WAYS TO COLLECT FEEDBACK

REFERENCE CHAPTER 5: THINK BIG, START SMALL, SCALE FAST

Hack #21: How any business starter can create a sales system to automatically build a quality sales pipeline without advertising?

1: CREATE A SALES SYSTEM TO ATTRACT, LINE-UP AND SCHEDULE

2: THE MORE YOU OFFER, THE MORE LEADS YOU'LL GENERATE

3: A SALES SYSTEM IS A SERIES OF LOGICAL STEPS

4: OFFER INFORMATION IN DIFFERENT FORMATS

5: THE SELF-LIQUIDATING OFFER

REFERENCE CHAPTER 6: WHAT TO SELL AND HOW TO SELL IT

Hack #22: Target your most appropriate market and exclude the others

1. Pre-existing market.

2. An entirely new market.

3. Existing market with low prices.

4. Existing market with new niche offerings.

REFERENCE CHAPTER 6: WHAT TO SELL AND HOW TO SELL IT

Hack #23: How to create custom assets to demonstrate your very tight market match

Create 'explainer videos' to demonstrate how you get things done in the field of your experience.

REFERENCE CHAPTER 6: WHAT TO SELL AND HOW TO SELL IT

Hack #24: Systematize your business and sell licenses for quick cash and rolling income

When you review operating processes, write them down. Most miss this whole, free, income stream.

REFERENCE CHAPTER 6: WHAT TO SELL AND HOW TO SELL IT

Hack #25: How to get to know who your top 20% target customers really are

Look for repeat customers or customers who only buy premium products.

REFERENCE CHAPTER 6: WHAT TO SELL AND HOW TO SELL IT

Hack #26: What can you outsource to ensure that you have a passive income?

License parts of your business and sell licenses. Easy cash wins.

REFERENCE CHAPTER 6: WHAT TO SELL AND HOW TO SELL IT

Hack #27: How to convert customers into clients to ensure your income grows and grows

Find out why customers buy, what else they buy, who from and how much.

REFERENCE CHAPTER 7: CONVERT CUSTOMERS TO CLIENTS

Hack #28: How does your tailor provide insights into cultivating professionalism?

The focus is on building rapport and getting to know clients in order to ensure the whole process is tailored to match client needs.

REFERENCE CHAPTER 7: CONVERT CUSTOMERS TO CLIENTS

Hack #29: How to use the 80:20 rule to pull out the most lucrative clients

Identify who the top 20% of customers are by their spending patterns

REFERENCE CHAPTER 7: CONVERT CUSTOMERS TO CLIENTS

Hack #30: Learn the best way to manage difficult, loss-making clients.

Eliminate them. Block their access. If you need to, you can explain next time they order you have no services that will suit them.

REFERENCE CHAPTER 7: CONVERT CUSTOMERS TO CLIENTS

Hack #31: Outsource cash and credit management if you want to sleep better at night

Hire a bank for sales discounting services

REFERENCE CHAPTER 7: CONVERT CUSTOMERS TO CLIENTS

Hack #32: Why must you keep your costs low? To preserve profits!

Do not buy anything unless someone forces you with a gun to your head.

REFERENCE CHAPTER 7: CONVERT CUSTOMERS TO CLIENTS

Hack #33: Apply the agile process to your business

Create a minimum bare bone product or service. Create quickly, so you can focus more time on finding out what customers really want.

REFERENCE CHAPTER 8: MASSIVE OPPORTUNITIES FOR SERVICE BUSINESSES

Hack #34: How to find your first, or next customer

Seek potential customers, speak directly, and ask for the business.

REFERENCE CHAPTER 9: HOW TO ASK FOR NEW BUSINESS

Hack #35: Ask questions to convert customers to clients

Ask customers about their future as well as current needs, and ask them about their hopes and dreams.

REFERENCE CHAPTER 9: HOW TO ASK FOR NEW BUSINESS

Hack #36: How to sell without being 'salesy'

Talk to people about everyday subjects, in a normal manner. Take a genuine interest in them.

REFERENCE CHAPTER 9: HOW TO ASK FOR NEW BUSINESS

Hack #37: Why and how you should spend time focused on your client's favorite subject

Conversations must start and be about them if you want to develop maximum rapport.

REFERENCE CHAPTER 9: HOW TO ASK FOR NEW BUSINESS

Hack #38: How to develop and roll out your very first sales system

Develop an on-boarding customer questionnaire. Offer it to prospects to complete.

REFERENCE CHAPTER 9: HOW TO ASK FOR NEW BUSINESS

Hack #39: How to see through the eyes of your customer

Create an avatar of whom your typical prospective customer is and what drives them.

REFERENCE CHAPTER 10: HOW TO WRITE AN AD FOR YOUR BUSINESS

Hack #40: Why should you get to know whom you are targeting?

You should find it a lot easier to resonate with them and with you. This can only help them to ultimately like you too.

REFERENCE CHAPTER 10: HOW TO WRITE AN AD FOR YOUR BUSINESS

Hack #41: How you save time by following the classic ad structure.

Following an ad-structure blueprint will save you time and energy as you will be totally focused on the steps to be completed.

REFERENCE CHAPTER 10: HOW TO WRITE AN AD FOR YOUR BUSINESS

Hack #42: Which works best? Long or short copy?

Both are good. Long copy takes advantage of space. It is usually associated with direct marketing. Where you are selling off a page or letter, and nowadays, the web too, page size is not a limitation. Short copy is better than nothing when space is limited.

REFERENCE CHAPTER 10: HOW TO WRITE AN AD FOR YOUR BUSINESS

Chapter 12:
Next Steps

We established the number one thing to focus on is to acquire a customer.

We referred to the key benefits a customer delivers to you. We demonstrated how a customer is the one thing necessary to enable you to describe what you do as a business and not a hobby. Just knowing this is all most people need to know when in start-up mode, yet there is more.

The requirement for a customer is not ordinarily the first thing start-up entrepreneurs usually think about. We often get caught up in the weeds of setting up and preparing to start a business. Or the sexy technology or the skills required to do what we need to do. These remain things we are rightly thrilled by. Yet customers, merely demand results.

Many start-ups make big errors pursuing the dream of the ideal vision. It is customers who correctly represent the unique group of people who can help you to actively transform your vision into reality. So, the quicker you get a customer, the quicker you can check your vision is something customers will want to buy. At any stage, you may discover you have to alter your approach to transform your vision into reality, and most of us appreciate the feedback.

Everyone will agree we never have enough time or money.

We all want more. Yet, a customer can provide us with more money too. What is interesting is when we focus on a customer, we tend to not focus on other things, nearly all of which are distractions. A customer is the key to providing you with all you need and so much more.

Over time, as your start-up matures and engages more customers, your customer objectives are likely to evolve. Initially, you are unknown and unique, and, after a while, your business will become solid and dependable. A start-up entrepreneur needs to prepare for the changes over time.

You must learn to spend some time developing the habit of creating assets. Customers are themselves assets, too. These can be managed for your business to develop your IP and market positioning. The continuous, ongoing development of assets will ultimately assist you to demonstrate why you are the best choice for your customers to invest in. Where possible, assets should be shareable. They should also, in a practical way, be capable of going viral to spread the word and encourage excitement in the market.

You will need to change and adapt

You may start with one type of customer that you find easy to satisfy, who will generate short-term cash and secure you the time you need. Optimistically, you will satisfy enough customers to fund the subsequent stage of the business. This achievement should allow you to pivot to the type of customer more faithful to your ideal vision of what your business is about. The path to success is not inevitably straight.

As you start to acquire your initial customer (s) you take the time to work with them closely to make sure you are capable of faithfully delivering what they desire. It is preferable to over-deliver to ensure they are completely delighted. You might start picking up testimonials or develop the ability to craft use cases or, with permission, publish a customer authorized testimonial and case study.

As time progresses, not only will your offer evolve and develop, as you find new and additional market opportunities. You will additionally want to develop repeatable, reliable, and low-cost sales systems and processes to entice new customers to you. At the same time, you will also learn to identify your premium customers and work on a similarly reliable, scalable method to convert customers to clients.

Successively, growth will put pressure on other parts of the business, including pressure to increase overheads and strengthen cash flow. You will determine more and better ways to finance sales, based on your experience of client behavior. All these issues need to be carefully managed as the business moves out of start-up mode and on into the future.

Over time, you will determine new and innovative ways to place stories and assets into the marketplace.

You will need to get better at over delivering and you will determine more about who you are for. You will know more about the marketplace you provide the best fit with and why customers buy from you. In this way, you will find it easier to generate more sales and grow.

You will start developing a market reputation. Perhaps in an emerging market, perhaps in a new niche of an existing market. You will understand more about your market type and positioning. You will discover ways to enhance your position. Your focus will narrow toward a group of potential customers who are both plentiful and open to doing business with you. They likewise will find it is straightforward to appreciate you positively.

Competence, confidence, and capability

Over time your business should grow and grow.

The more you customize your customer offering, the more likely you will convert customers to clients. You will start acquiring longer term contracts, with some clients placing until cancelled or subsequent, rolling orders. With this level of maturity, you will find some banks will start to look favorably toward you. They may indeed provide financial services to fund your customer and client needs, which will be of considerable assistance and help to finance growth.

In the short term, do not expect too much financial help.

Some help generally becomes available as you demonstrate initial clients and longer term, repeat business.

You deserve a massive pat on the back for succeeding this far. Most people never hear the words 'you are doing well' or to be congratulated. Most merely think you are doing something you ought to undertake, and besides, you are making money from it, aren't you?

Allow me then to congratulate you on your success. I know how tough it is and how straightforward it may sound and yet how difficult it can be.

Thank you

Do make sure you register on the books accompanying website at *https://TheAuthorityFigure.com/* to ensure you acquire more insights into how your business can work better.

You will also receive the most recent updates and access to a range of bonus materials, videos and resources as discussed in this book. You will in addition receive updates by email on my upcoming books in this series.

In conclusion, thank you for reading this book. I hope you have as much fun running your business as I have had running mine.

If this topic interests you, make sure to sign up for my free newsletter https://theauthorityfigure.substack.com/ where I have more to share.

I hope you have enjoyed reading this book. Would you please leave a review on Amazon at https://amzn.to/3vpEFWF. Thank you. Reviews help other readers find the book. You would provide a great service to this author and future readers.

CPSIA information can be obtained
at www.ICGtesting.com
Printed in the USA
LVHW090744020623
748370LV00043B/539